Fred Vermorel was born in London on September 2 194█
had met in de Gaulle's wartime army and settled in Engla█
media and history at Harrow School of Art, the Sorbonne
London and University of Sussex. He has been a painter a█
about the history of photography and suburbia as well as several pioneering best
sellers on pop highly acclaimed by, among others, the *New Statesman*, *Le Monde* and
the international rock press.

He is particularly interested in the art of pop – that newest and possibly most
potent of all the arts, and this book, as well as exploring the unique power of Kate
Bush's music and performance, probes in witty and affectionate detail the secrets of
her image and erotic fascination.

Back cover shows Pebmarsh churchyard where generations of Kate's ancestors are buried.

© Copyright 1983 F. Vermorel
First published 1983 Omnibus Press
(A division of Book Sales Limited)
Book designed by Fred Vermorel
Production by Judy Vermorel
Artwork by Alan Lenton
Typeset by DahDah Ltd, London

Exclusive distributors:
Book Sales Limited
8/9 Frith Street, London W1V 5TZ, England
Music Sales Pty Limited
GPO Box 3304, Sydney, NSW 2001, Australia
To the Music Trade Only:
Music Sales Limited
8/9 Frith Street, London W1V 5TZ, England

ISBN 0.7119.0152.X
UK Order No. OP 42035

Printed in Gt. Britain
by Blantyre Printing & Binding Co. Limited

"The communication of music is very like making love."

Kate Bush

"If you put yourself into the icon, the icon will speak to you. . . It has a magic effect."

Jung

To Kate and Joe Bush,
for their courage.

the secret history of
KATE BUSH
(& the strange art of pop)

Fred Vermorel

Omnibus Press
London/New York/Sydney/Cologne

I

We recognised her as we always do stars. A face "clicks", happens, transfigures anonymity. As the eye jumps to a pretty face in a crowd, the word "sex" on a page. So decisively it seems a star is *born*. But not out of labour. Rather as a flying saucer crash-landed on earth. Gleaming mysterious and seamless in its crater. Surrounded by excited cameramen and fenced off by stern authority. A worldwide object of speculation: Gee! Is there anyone – anything – inside? And is it friendly?

So she burst through the telly in early '78. All wrists and lisp and dimples, all sweet and clever, all arms like water flowing over stones, as clean and delicious as a scoop of avocado pear. The suburbs breathed again. Fresh air after punk's foul blast. And very soon very famous. A hit, a gold, a number one. Introduced to gentry. An institution. Snap, crackle and pop. A campaign of champagne. Prizes, encore!, and: who the hell does she think she is? "The most photographed woman in Britain."

Then she disappeared.

And destroyed her talent. For two years worked to wreck her facility and build something more interesting in the ruins. As every artist has to. And has taken pop production its furthest yet. As frank as Cliff, as crisp as the Floyd, as potent as the Pistols. And her work's now as sharp and inspired as David Hockney's (which it resembles). Only more important. For Hockney's art is defunct: fine art painting. But hers is the only art which really counts today. Not pop art, but the art of pop.

A strange, could be dangerous art. Crazy Kate, pop witch. She exorcises our madness. Lives and projects myths she can't always control. Or understand.

Also an unusual person with unusual reflexes – a welcome antidote to most

of us. How did she come about? I followed the fragile chances and distillation which produced her and her art and realized how nearly she never made it – for which we'd be the poorer. And also followed her appearance through her folklore: Kate sphinx, Kate harlequin, Kate harlot... A history of our expectations and recognition.

> *"Fear cautions me, 'Remain a stranger,'*
> *Yet longing urges, 'Do not wait.'*
> *Her eyes spell secrecy and danger,*
> *Yet they are my dark stars of fate."*
> *(Heine, "Katherine")*

II

They buried women alive. We dig up the skeletons still contorted with panic. As feuding and family-mad as any Sicilian, their heads full of tense concentric art: tortured bloodlines and the gaze of skulls. They loved riddles, feared hauntings and gave their swords psychopathic identities. The Romans, no pacifists, noted their "fierce and terrible glance".

Frig was their goddess of love (hence "Friday" which was dedicated to her). Hated by Christians as "that foul goddess Venus". Wife to Odin, the father god, and mother to all other gods. And fertility and earth goddess: Mother Earth. Priests announced her visitations whereupon the community hid all its iron objects and weapons and made merry and love until she left. Then the ceremonial wagon she'd arrived in was thrown in a bog. And the slaves who performed this ritual were drowned.

Her ancestors were part of the second wave of Saxon invasion around 500 AD. They slipped out of the mouth of the German River Elbe in a ship like a rearing swan, heavy with household goods, and alive and stinking with dogs, pigs, sheep, cattle, horses. They rowed for several days and nights with the chant of oarsmen, scrambling children, smoke of cooking fires. Then reached the Essex coast just above Blackwater where they swung into the River Colne's wide triangular mouth.

Two miles up river was a busy Saxon town clustered around the ruins of Roman Colchester. Here they equipped and orientated themselves. Then they followed the Colne winding inland through primaeval forest until they found a high gravel hill strategically overlooking river and woodland which they called "a healthy place" (Halstead) and settled.

Some time later her people moved a few miles away into a forest clearing – possibly near the older settlement of Wickham St Paul. They kept bees for honey, wax candles and mead, and hunted small game, wild berries, mushrooms and nuts. And herbs to make medicine and magic.

For Bush is an Anglo Saxon name for those who lived in (or by or at) the bush. Hence Aluric Busch (11th century), Henry del Busk (13th century), Roland atte Bushe (14th century). And bush then meant forest. So her ancestors were Anglo Saxon forest dwellers.

But which forest, where? A labour of love was needed. No sweat. Kate Bush! What a site for excavation, research, reverie! Unpick red tape with a lover's care, track her by the dry white flash of Xerox, break the dust of paper bundles, copy handwritten notes from cardboard boxes in the Society of Genealogists' Tweedale Room, focus microfiches from the mad Mormon Computer Index of Christenings: Burton . . . Bury . . . Busby . . . Bush!, track backwards and forwards and sideways and madways from her first certain ancestor, born in 1769, through the scatter in time and England of Bushes against migration and history, by manorial rolls, surname studies, parish and dissenting registers, army muster rolls and paylists, electoral registers and censuses, War Office and criminal records, and ancient field names: Bush Cranny, Bush Meadow, Bush End. . .

"Bush". It comes with a pout of wet-lip cheesecake promise. Say "Bush" and you kiss. *"Bouche"* is mouth in sensual French. And pussy is risqué English. From the bump of B to the shush of Babooshka, Bush baby, Bush me. Bush girl, I'm Bush crazy, lush Bush and I'll gush Bush. And take Kate, Kate conjugate, Kate fashionplate. . .

Kate Kodak slowly configures in a thousand acid baths under the red light of dark rooms. Bulbs pop into pop pix. A face stained in newsprint. Phantom flesh in TV's liquid bubble. A crackle of intelligence in pop's histrionic babble. But her face also crystallises around her absence. Kate Bush evaporates under our million eyes. We stare at the star who turns to stone. For *celebrities are dead people*. But she deserves better. Bring her back to life. Create Kate.

Starting in this tiny corner of north-east Essex where all my research led –

around the town of Halstead and the unusual little village of Pebmarsh. Where her family seems to have lived for 1,400 years!

In winter, the omnipresent Essex sky and landscape carries voices with uncanny precision. Fields smoke with mist and ivy encrusted trees point broken black fingers. But spring ripens chestnut buds fat and sticky as a man's penis, while green and birdsong shimmers and furtive grouse scuttle over lanes and swallows play dizzy tag under my parked car. Then four ducks pop importantly out of a ditch to quack single file over a field towards Pebmarsh.

Pebmarsh lies at the centre of narrow lanes which twist around Spoons Hall, Marvels Garden, World's End Farm, Rakes Hall and the old Blue Pales Farm. The few modern semis and bungalows hardly change the feel of a village haemorrhaged in the 1880s by the collapse of its strange industrial adventure and then forgotten. No electricity reached here until the mid-40s and no mains water or sewerage until the early 60s.

Some authorities derive "Pebmarsh" from "peas marsh": a marsh where peas were grown. But Pete Daws, the village publican, thinks "Peb" is a corruption of *"ped"* for foot signifying the (probably Roman) footpath which forded the tiny brook cutting lazily through the village before it winds into the Colne.

The village is scattered in a T-shape with its church, St John the Baptist's, at centre. Go right and the road rises steeply past the new red brick school to the war memorial and forbidding granite rectory at Cross End. Left, you cross a little bridge over the brook to the 17th century village pub, the Kings Head, and a bright red telephone box. Down, and Mill Lane leads you to the millhouse and site of the old silk mill.

Today it's a picturesque haven. In July butterflies confetti the bleached forecourt of the Kings Head while sunlight from an open door filters through an aquarium peace of fag smoke and alcohol to lick the dimples in copper table tops. You might expect faded red crushed sofas and an oriental blaze of bedpans and flying ducks, soup ladles, hunting horns, horseshoes and pudding bowls. But Eileen Daws has also laid on a model galleon and ship's bell, a stark African shield and pale rag doll, and gold and red painted dried rushes explode in gloomy corners while a brass bowl of geraniums is decorated in pink and mauve bows like a gorgeously fat little girl.

This part of Essex went from forest into a modern field system without an intervening period of peasant smallholdings. And the name Bush also suggests her Saxon ancestors were employed to destroy their own habitat by clearing forest. This was the great Saxon work which turned England into open countryside. So they were never serfs, but Saxon coerls and foresters, then forest workers. And after that labourers, ploughing, sowing and harvesting the fields they'd created.

Mud was the Historical Fact which preoccupied them. Not much mud in history books. But Essex mud is legendary. Mud dragged and filled their boots, churned and clogged wheels, resisted, slewed and stuck ploughs, caked around tools, went creamy in rain, bubbled in bogs and froze like iron. Mud cottage floors, mud paths, ditches, banks. . . And mud claimed them on that springy hillside cemetery, topped with its gaunt 13th century church, where I walked over the bones of Susan Bush, dead at one in 1873 of "marasmus" (starvation), and old John Bush, dead at 77 in 1846 – Kate's great-great-great-grandfather.

Before the 19th century many farm labourers lived in sin without bothering to baptise their children. And Pebmarsh ministers were an idle and temperamental lot, little interested in hounding miscreant Bushes to altar or font. Even so, in 1695 Abraham Bush had his son baptised Abraham in the village of Little Maplestead, a satellite of Pebmarsh – and 200 years later a pivotal village in our Bush fortunes. And when the Pebmarsh registers do improve and begin to get comprehensive, around the mid-18th century, they reveal a whole tribe of Bushes already living in and around Pebmarsh. Other earlier records also show Pebmarsh was *the* Bush village for many miles around. (And today there's not one Bush left.)

We can piece together enough to show that John Bush, Kate's first certain ancestor born in 1769 (whom I shall call John 1), married an Esther (also spelt "Easter") Fincham in 1794. John 1 was probably the son of William and Rebecca Bush who also had a daughter Jane. Esther bore John 1 a daughter (also called Jane) in March 1795, but then lost two sons (both called John) in infancy before she herself died in 1809. So John was a widower of 44 when he married (or set up home with) the 22 year old Hannah in around 1813.

John and Hannah waited until March 31 1820 before having their first three children baptized: John, 7, Hannah, 5, and Jemima of two months. After that they had Sophia in 1822 and Henry (Kate's great-great-grand-father) in May 1824. Then twins Sarah and William, in 1827. Hannah died only 13, Jemima 14, Sarah 18 months old, and William after five weeks.

The Bushes were scum. Growers of food and keepers of cattle and sheep whose children died of starvation and malnutrition.

"It is difficult to find words for the degradation which the coming of industrial society brought to the English country labourer. . . Everything conspired to impoverish and to demoralise them. They lost what little traditional right and security they had, and gained instead not even the theoretical hope which capitalism held out to the urban labourer, the legal equality of rights in the liberal society, the possibility of ceasing to be a proletarian. Instead, another, less human, more unequal hierarchy closed in upon them – the farmer who talked to them like a squire, the squire who drove them out for partridge and hares, the collective conspiracy of the village rich who took their commons, and gave them instead their charity in return for their servility, and on whose whim depended their livelihood. They did not even sell their birthright for a mess of pottage. They simply lost it."

(Hobsbaum and Rudé, *Captain Swing*)

Some men escaped through the army. And military records show at least three Pebmarsh Bushes joined the East Suffolk 63rd Foot (nicknamed the Bloodsuckers). William Bush joined in 1814 but was demobilised only two years later when he married Elizabeth Mole and settled in Pebmarsh to raise nine children. Lucky William, for John Bush (not John 1) joined only 14 years old in 1817 and served 27 years, gradually being undermined by 30 tropical illnesses until contracting dyspepsia, when he was invalided out to the military hospital at Chatham. The third, Edward Bush, who was probably the brother of John 1, served in the West Indies, America, and around the Mediterranean for 15 years from 1807, becoming a corporal and leaving at 38 "worn out in the service". He is described in his discharge papers as "five foot four and a half inches tall" and dark haired, with hazel eyes and "a fresh complexion". (Rather like Kate.)

But then Pebmarsh was suddenly and dramatically transformed by the whim of an eccentric philanthropist and adventurer.

George Courtauld, born in 1761, was the son of a French Huguenot family exiled to England. He travelled the US in his youth, adventuring among Redskins and speculating in land before returning to England with an Irish wife and two children. A passionate anti-monarchist and revolutionary, he

Over the page. Top left: Kate inside the 350 year old East Wickham Farmhouse where she was brought up (London Express). Top right: The South Ockenden Wesleyan Chapel when it was frequented by Kate's grandparents. Sermons were sometimes interrupted by shouts of "No brother! No brother!". Bottom left: Pebmarsh in the 1880s, looking down Mill Lane where Hannah and Jemima Bush walked to work every morning at six. Bottom right; The King's Head c. 1890 where the inquest on Henry Bush took place.

dreamed of "forming . . . a union of capital and labour on terms mutually advantageous".

Pebmarsh was then a remote, inaccessible and backward village. No one knows why Courtauld had the apparently mad idea of building a silk mill here. He turned the existing flour mill into a factory for "throwing" silk (twisting raw silk into thread), built a millhouse and several workers' cottages, trained the population and generally, as his daughter Sophia recalled proudly, turned "a wilderness into a scene of tasteful comfort and extended usefulness". The village grew from 423 inhabitants in 1801 to 683 in 1851. And by 1840 an Essex directory counted two bakers, four shop-keepers, three beerhouses (not counting the Kings Head), one policeman, two butchers, a tailor and six other various tradespeople.*

Pebmarsh silk mill (demolished in 1901) was the apparently mad adventure of eccentric visionary George Courtauld. It transformed the village.

*It's quite likely considering the mortality rate that without Courtauld's adventure Kate's line wouldn't have survived. His factory supplied Pebmarsh and its environs with a small but crucial margin of affluence.

No sooner was the Pebmarsh mill finished than George Courtauld went on to build other silk mills and by his restless schemes nearly bankrupted his family. The business was commandeered by his sons, and George, a better dreamer than businessman, returned to the US full of new ideas to improve humanity, only to die there of a fever in 1823. His enterprise eventually grew into today's Courtauld empire. But the original Pebmarsh mill was bought by two brothers, Edward and Henry Rodick, silk merchants from the City of London, and their family owned and managed it for the next 70 years.*

So the Industrial Revolution's traumas and riches reached Pebmarsh before surrounding villages, making it a busy little island of modernity, where the Bushes, especially Bush women (most men remained labourers), made the huge and irreversible leap into the time, values and logic of clocks and wages. Pebmarsh people became a byword in the district for "sharpness" and "city ways" and Pebmarsh women notorious for their fierce and organised independence.

> *"I knew her by her angry air,*
> *Her bright black eyes, her bright black hair,*
> *Her rapid laughters wild and shrill,*
> *As laughters of the woodpecker. . .*
> *'Tis Kate – she sayeth what she will:*
> *For Kate hath an unbridled tongue,*
> *Clear as the twanging of a harp. . ."*
> (Tennyson, "Kate")

On September 1 1846 John 1 died after a six months illness they called "dry gangrene of the foot" (probably blood poisoning).

One year earlier on November 15 1845 Henry Bush, then 21, had married the 20 year old Esther Jarvice. They became Kate's great-great-grand-parents. Esther came from the nearby town of Earls Colne but they settled in Pebmarsh where Esther had her first child, George, in August 1846. She

---

*The Rodick line has vanished utterly. Hoping to find some candid reminiscences from these Victorian bachelor brothers I followed them through several subsequent childless marriages into a biological cul-de-sac. Even their London Blackheath home has disappeared. And the futuristic Nat. West. skyscraper now looms from the site of their former city offices. Pebmarsh also forgot them and Archibald Rodick's dying gift of cash to former mill girls in 1934 is wrongly attributed to the more glamorous Courtauld connection. The only thing the Rodicks seem to have passed on is Archibald's stamp collection. But maybe in someone's attic. . .?

also had Hannah in 1850, Rachel in 1854, Jemima in 1857 and then on September 12 1859 John 2, Kate's great-grandfather.

No.	When Married.	Name and Surname.	Age.	Condition.	Rank or Profession.	Residence at the Time of Marriage.	Father's Name and Surname.	Rank or Profession of Father.
49	December 15	Henry Bush / Ester Jarvis	full / 20	Bachelor / Spinster	Labourer / —	Pebmarsh / Pebmarsh	John Bush / George Jarvis	Labourer / Labourer

1843. Marriage solemnized at Pebmarsh Church in the Parish of Pebmarsh in the County of Essex

Married in the Parish Church according to the Rites and Ceremonies of the Church of England by me, Philip Brett

This Marriage was solemnized between us, Henry Bush {his mark} X / Ester Jarvice {her ...} X — in the Presence of us, John Johnson {his mark} X / Sophia Johnson {her —} X

Henry Bush's whole world was Pebmarsh. For parish boundaries meant more to Victorian labourers than county or national ones. The parish defined and bound him by law and custom. And his only social security was the parish chest. Outside Pebmarsh Henry was nobody.

Most of the Pebmarsh relief papers have vanished. But one notebook survives, covering 1831-3. William Bush (the ex-soldier) is now living in a tiny cottage with his numerous family and makes a record number of applications for "clothing for a bed", a boy's smock, shoes (four times), more allowance (twice) and "a doctor for wife". By no means the only Bush wanting: John Bush applied for fuel, Edward for "something being ill" and a "Widow Bush" for nursing Elizabeth Coote in her home. These appeals were heard before village notables who might turn them down for a whim.

For Henry the countryside was a hostile place of harsh and poorly paid work. Even the hedges could seem to take his enemies' part. George Trendell, recalling the turn of the century, told us Pebmarsh farmers might give a labourer "a hedge to cut for his firewood, you see, that was a present for him. And they used to say, 'Oh, gave him a hedge that was absolutely no good, the poor old joker.'"

George Trendell also recalled Pebmarsh families "used to *live*, but if they had turnips for a meal they had turnips. They didn't have turnips and a mixture of all sorts of things". And an Essex labourer, looking back to Henry's time stated that

"for months at a time he had existed upon nothing but a diet of bread and onions, washed down, when he was lucky, with a little small-beer. These onions he ate until they took the skin off the roof of his mouth, blistering it to whiteness, after which he was obliged to soak them in salt to draw 'the virtue' out of them. They had no tea, but his wife imitated the appearance of that beverage by soaking a burnt crust of bread in boiling water. On this diet he became so feeble that the reek of the muck which it was his duty to turn, made

Pebmarsh Rectory in July 1842. The rector of Pebmarsh, Harbottle Grimston, would creep around the village at nights making notes on his parishioners.

him sick and faint; and often, he said, he would walk home at night from the patch of ground where he grew his onions and some other vegetables, with swimming head and uncertain feet."

(Rider Haggard, Rural England)

The church focused official Pebmarsh. An ecclesiastical census for 1851 reckons an average Sunday morning service mustered 104 and the afternoon service 332 – three quarters of the village! For much of the 19th century its rectors were the two Harbottle Grimstons. The first Harbottle Grimston lived with his five unmarried sisters, famous for their bright red hair. He never married and had the odd habit of creeping around the village at night making notes on parishioners who stayed up late. By the end of his life he "appeared to have totally lost his intellects". The second Harbottle Grimston was a more convivial and robust figure who rode lustily to hounds and played a mean game of cricket for his villagers. Sam Raymond was the sexton in Henry's day, a white haired old tartar who patrolled services with a long stave and "if he found any lads sleeping, or otherwise misbehaving, he brought it down on their heads. I recollect well hearing the whacks".

There was also an unofficial Pebmarsh which seethed with the intimacies and disputes of shared poverty and sharp dramas of petty theft and poaching. This Pebmarsh centred on the several local beerhouses which (unlike the Kings Head) were run by the labourers' (roughly) social equals. Edward Bush and his wife Hannah ran one opposite the rectory at Cross End in the little whitewashed cottage, now the residence of a Halstead dentist. They raised themselves from labouring and their son Charles trained as a servant. When Hannah died suddenly of apoplexy in 1859 and Edward followed her in 1860, Charles and his wife Sarah took over and expanded into a brewery and pork butchers.

These beerhouses worried farmers and gentry who saw them as hothouses of sedition. No doubt they sometimes bristled with plans to burn a hayrick or fix a gamekeeper. But mostly rang with a unpolitical revelry (beer was cheap and potent) and singing with melodion and tambourine, and dancing in which "the amazing amount of sound. . . [the dancer] got out of the floor and his hobnailed boots, were the chief features of the performance".

Unofficial Pebmarsh became official once a year when the village went wild for its fair every St John the Baptist's day (June 24). So boisterously that in 1787 a spoilsport faction had tried to ban it. But not unusual then. As a judicial report intoned:

"... many unlawful games and plays, besides drinking and other debaucheries are encouraged and carried on under pretence of meeting at such fairs to the great increase of vice and immorality and to the debauching and ruin of servants, apprentices and other unwary people and many riots, tumults and other disorders are occasioned thereby."

The Kings Head forecourt was filled with stalls selling gingernuts, bulls-eyes, gooseberry pies, ribbons, "ballads, spices, penny toys, gown pieces, garters, peppermint sticks, china and watches". Also peepshows, fire-eaters, amazing "fat ladies" and "living skeletons", etc.

Inevitably ending in brawls. For Pebmarsh was a violent place. George Trendell recalls of the labourers: "They were always fighting. Ooh I've seen some terrible fighting. I can remember there was a fight and I heard the chap hit the road and then of course he couldn't get up so they carried him away to the pump and pumped on him till he came round and then set him up fighting again."

In this society Henry Bush was king. For Henry had become a notorious and violent village drunkard. He was often drunk, it was said, "for days on end" and once terrified Esther by having "convulsive fits in bed" which a doctor put down to "intemperance".

"God has covered your bones with flesh. Your flesh is soft and warm. In your flesh there is blood. . .

How easy it would be to hurt your poor little body!

If it were to fall into the fire, it would be burned up. If hot water were thrown upon it, it would be scalded. If it were to fall into deep water, and not be taken out very soon, it would be drowned. If a great knife were run through your body, the blood would come out. If a great box were to fall on your head, your head would be crushed. If you were to fall out of the window, your neck would be broken."

(Anon, *The Peep of Day* – an extremely popular Victorian reading primer.)

Henry's children attended the village school in a cottage next to the church where they would have been the butt of their father's notoriety as well as enduring the routine savagery of Victorian school life. Most labourers' children were absent as often as they dared, illicitly hoeing or harvesting with their parents. They were also often sick as a school diary (started in 1896) shows, noting: "much sickness", "had to send two infants home suffering from ringworm", "sickness prevails in the village", etc, and in September 1900 the whole school closed for nine weeks because of "bad attendance and sickness".

Pebmarsh schoolchildren around the turn of the century outside the village store where Rachel Bush bought her first maid's uniform.

When George and John left school at 11 in the 1860s they took up the dismal lot of farm labourers. But Hannah and Jemima went to work in the Rodick's silk mill – a three storey, whitewashed building three minutes from their cottage. Here they worked from six in the morning to six at night in the constant thunder and dust of the steam engine or machines twisting bales of raw silk into thread which was then wound on to bobbins. At around 10 shillings and 4 pence a week, the wages were quite good and mill girls sometimes shocked their betters by turning up to church in unwonted finery. But discipline was harsh and in one nearby mill included fines and beatings as well as wearing a dunce's cap for being wasteful.

Esther Bush worked at home, straw plaiting (to supply the Victorian fashion for straw hats and bonnets). Also a fairly well paid occupation which thrived in this part of Essex:

> "Whenever you went into a cottage, you saw a bowl or pail of water standing, in which these little yellow strips were steeped, and the smell of the straw (to which a dash of brimstone was also added) pervaded all the humble dwelling."

But school had taught Rachel Bush to read and write (unlike her brother John 2). And maybe also to dream. For rather than work in the mill, Rachel went into domestic service. This was extremely tedious and gruelling work, but it *was* a way up. A way to break through what was a vast – and to us unimaginable – gap in social and material culture. So Rachel was kitted out at the village general store with a uniform (bought on tick and paid back a penny a week). And left Pebmarsh with her belongings for the short journey to Wakes Colne. And she later became the first of Kate's line to pull herself out of the Pebmarsh mud.

But for labourers, work was scarce. Parish records show farmers took turns to employ men on fairly useless tasks for minimum wages to keep them off relief (the normal average wage was around 11 shillings a week). For a man with three working daughters and a working wife this must have been humiliating. No wonder Henry turned increasingly to drink, waxing eloquent and fierce in local beerhouses in his brightly coloured waistcoat, collarless shirt, corduroy trousers and bowler hat.

In July 1871 Hannah Bush, now 23, married William Hicks, a labourer of 25, also from Pebmarsh. This did nothing to improve Henry's temper for we next find him in November 1872 engaged in a "scrimmage" in Mr Clark's tap room where he "got a black eye".

It is now Monday December 2 1872. Henry is unemployed. He lies in bed until around 10 when Esther's nagging drives him from the cottage. Will he be looking for work? Yes, yes, woman. But no sooner is Henry out the door than he makes for Lumley's beerhouse to breakfast on a pint of ale. And by 11, a scandalised Mrs Creffield discovers him "already the worse for drink". After which Henry visits another beerhouse.

Then at four o'clock that afternoon, about four miles away in Wakes Colne, Rachel Bush was startled by a commotion and Henry staggered into her mistress's kitchen. He was quite drunk and probably asked Rachel for money. She may have given him a drink – which she later denied – but certainly saw him off quite sharply. Henry declared he was returning to Pebmarsh. But never got there.

For an event intervened which was to plunge our Bushes to their lowest point ever.

III

"O tell me where did Katy live
And what did Katy do?
And was she very fair and young,
And yet so wicked, too?
Did Katy love a naughty man,
Or kiss more cheeks than one?
I warrant Katy did no more
Than many a Kate has done."
(Oliver Wendell Holmes)

Kate: "Fred – what happened to us?"
Fred: "Could have been your disposition."
Kate: "Or maybe your ego."

(Cole Porter, *Kiss Me Kate*)

"Catherine Bush". Mum and dad's spoony blueprint for a daughter. Some authorities derive the name from the Latin for "pure", others from the Greek for "torture".

She chose the more robust diminutive. "Catherine" swoons across the page. "Kate" stands up. No Saint Kate. But ten Catherines! Of Alexandria: tortured, broken on the Catherine wheel and decapitated. Of Siena with stigmata. Of Bologna: mystic bride of the infant Christ. Catherine De Palma: "subject to trances. . . visions and to assaults from invisible sources". And three of Henry VIII's six wives.

> "Where, then, can all the difference be?
>   Where? but between the K——C——:
> Between the graceful curving line
>   We now prefix to atherine,
> Which seems to keep, with mild police,
>   Those rebel syllables in peace,
> Describing, in the line of duty,
>   Both physical and moral beauty,
> And that impracticable K
>   Who led them all so much astray —
> Was never seen in black and white
>   A character more full of spite!
> That stubborn back, to bend unskilful,
>   So perpendicularly wilful!
> With angles hideous to behold,
>   Like the sharp elbows of a scold . . ."
> (Catherine Fanshawe, "The Letter K")

Kate gobs on the village green and shows her arse to the parson. A female outlaw in dozens of ballads, poems, stories and plays. And Shakespeare's Kate in *The Taming of the Shrew* comes from a tradition of vitriolic and violent Kate campaigners in the sex war. A *wilful woman.*

> Then Kate she rose in furious rage,
>   And at him she let blatter O,
> The poker tongs and ladle too,
>   On poor Will's head did rattle O.
> She cried You rogue are you begun
>   To starve me here already O?
> Is this the vow you made to me,
>   To keep me like a lady O.
>
>   . . .
>
> She broke his shins and tore his hair,
>   She made poor Will to wonder O:
> The pots and pans the stools and chairs,
>   About his head did thunder O.
>
> Will was na us'd in sic a fray,
>   He ran out-by for shelter O,

Crying Curse upon the fatal day
That I to Kate was halter'd O."
(Anonymous ballad)

Feminine nature, raw and unhusbanded. To be broken and tamed like a wild horse. The scold whipped and ducked. Bullied and starved by Petruchio into a "household Kate". Whose tongue even the Devil in Dvorak's opera, *Kate and the Devil,* can't take – and exiles her from hell! Who Cole Porter in *Kiss Me Kate* ("I Hate Men") has spanked into wifely submission.

And our own deputy headmaster of British rock'n'roll, John Peel, has also spanked Kate Bush by declaring rather grandly that he "can't take her seriously". John, who *has* taken seriously the simpering Claire Grogan of Altered Images, and Anabella – McLaren's creature whose image was contrived to evoke a Third World child prostitute.

Kate Bush is less easily patronised. Impossible to mould, obsessively independent, she writes her own songs, choreographs herself and designs her own videos, oversees her fan club, manages herself – even produces herself in the studio. Truly a woman with her own voice. Whose "Wuthering Heights" electrified the hit parade like the terrifying war cry ululation of Arab women.

And Hekate. Carnally explosive. Dazzling and sizzling. Kates beguile, draw, drown, ruin men:

"O did you not hear of Kate Kearney,
She lives on the banks of Killarney,
From the glance of her eye, shun danger and fly
For fatals the glance of Kate Kearney."
(Irish song)

Kate McCloud, a kept woman so absurdly luscious she turns Truman Capote's invention (for *Knave*) into a sticky meringue of superlatives. "Her loose hair, her dreaming head," moans our American. But André Maurois keeps his *savoir faire*:

"The ship rolls. The dark waters heave, then fall, in giant breathings. 'Mrs Wingate,' the Captain introduced. Pretty. A vigorous husband watched her respectfully. A Little Red Ridinghood dress, crimson scarf round the neck. A smile. 'Kate, darling,' says the husband. 'It's cocktail time.' She follows him.

. . .

'A Martini, darling?' 'No darling – a mint julep.' She lies full-length on the couch. Black and white dress. Perfect legs. 'I love poetry,' she tells me. 'I do so want to buy Verlaine. Is he good?'

. . .

A sports dress. Charming. Beige jumper with slanting brown lines. 'A French husband . . .' says Kate. 'What more does he do for his wife?' 'He tries to understand her, my dear Kate.' She runs her tongue over her lips. 'But there's nothing to understand,' she says, quite ingenuous, quite sincere."

("Kate")

"A Katy" was Scots dialect for a wanton and "a Kate" US slang for an *attractive* prostitute, and underworld jargon for "a smart, brazen-faced woman". Also *Kate Handcock,* anon, 1882, noted by Ashby, who once forced on to the game becomes "well content with her lot".

Because Kates either are dangerous company, or they keep it. Only the second Kate in literature:

> *"They banysshed prayer peas and sadnes*
> *And toke with them myrthe sporte and gladnes*
> *They wolde not have vertu ne yet devocyon*
> *But ryotte and revell with Joly Rebellyon*
> *They songe and daunsed full merely*
> *With swerynge and starynge heven hye."*
>
> . . .
>
> *"Here is Kate with the crooked fote*
> *That is Colfys daughter the dronken koke [cook]*
> *A lusty pye baker."*
> *(Cocke Lorell's bote – a saucy Tudor satire)*

And Kates use their charms to advantage. In the adventures of Tom and Jerry *(Life in London),* the scandalous 18th century best seller, Kate becomes Tom's own girl: "PROPRIETY, and even *character,* had been leaped over in order to gratify her AMBITION." Of all Edgar Wallace's spotless heroines, his Kate stands out:

" 'She is, I believe, the brains of the biggest criminal organisation in the world. Every member of the gang has been taken, but no evidence has ever been offered against Kate. She plans the big swindles and each one is bigger than the last – but never once have we traced the offence to her door.' "

(Edgar Wallace, *Kate plus 10*)

And in the end she marries the detective!

"Kate being pleas'd, wisht that her pleasure could

Indure as long as a buff jerkin would.
Content thee Kate, although thy pleasure wasteth
Thy pleasure's place like a buff jerkin lasteth.
For no buff jerkin hath bin oftner worne
Nor hat more scrapings, or more dressings borne."
(Sir John Davies)

In dialect, "Kate" was the darting wren and Cumbrian for a hare, and also the brambling finch which used to be caught for a singing bird.

"Kate rose up early as fresh as a lark,
Almost in time to see vanish the dark. . ."
(T Sturge Moore)

Wrote one Victorian: "There is something refreshing in this frankly practical specimen of girlhood, a breezy, freespoken heroine with no nonsense about her." And Charlotte Yonge had her *Countess Kate:* "tall, skinny and brown" with "loose rough waves of dark chestnut hair, large hazel eyes with blue whites" "and her slim, neatly-made foot was always a reproach to her for making such boisterous steps". Likewise Horace Stanton's American Kate Eldridge who "would have been a poor heroine for a novelist, for she was not 'a pale, fragile girl', and had no fainting fits in her composition, and was by no means a promising subject for consumption".

But such girls also alarmed. *Argosy* magazine's Katie "was the leader of the Row Boys, and a most potent Amazonian warrior . . . at the head of her well-organised forces. I see her now, with her long black unkempt hair streaming back upon the wind, and her dark, flashing eyes as she rushed into the fray; and she had at command a choice selection of expletives which none of our side would have dared to make use of . . ." Obviously a threat to propriety and order. So in many tales and moral tracts Kate appears as a cautionary heroine whose too free spirit is suitably crushed by a redeeming fall. A tradition culminating of course in Susan Coleridge's mean book, *What Katy Did,* where Katy, you remember, is crippled for being zestful and attractive.

In modern stories Kate is often a tomboy who teaches little boys a thing or two . . . who big boys lose sight of and men regret. A farmer's daughter I played with summers. She showed me her dad's gelignite hidden in a barn loft. We fought in haystacks. And one hot day sitting on a stile just before lunch she farted. I was astonished. I never knew girls could.

"Allie, call the children,
Call them from the green!

Allie calls, Allie sings,
*   Soon they run in:*
First there came
Tom and Madge,
*   Kate and I who'll not forget*
How we played by the water's edge
*   Till the April sun set."*
*   (Robert Graves, "Allie")*

IV

After leaving Rachel at Wakes Colne, Henry Bush took the quick way back to Pebmarsh along a little used track. No moon. Black sky, black mud, black mood. After two miles he saw the lights of Great Catley's Farm. With the freezing wind and that long walk, I don't know how drunk Henry could still have been but probably drunk enough to curse the dogs as he passed the gate and they probably cursed him back. He stumbled towards a sharp bend left, 150 yards on, before a dark grove of trees. The dogs were still barking distantly when Henry suddenly lost his grip on everything, the night, the stars, this story – he rolled to the edge of the page, his arms shot out, brambles split his face, he was tumbling and then crashed, completely winded, into a black hole.

Henry had missed his turn and fallen into a ditch.

I found that ditch. And one December evening in 1981 I recreated the incident.

Henry's Corner.

Pebmarsh.

SHOCKING DEATH FROM INTEMPERANCE.

Rachel Bush, Wakes Colne : Deceased was my father ; I saw him alive last on Monday about 4 o'cl ck in the afternoon, when he came to see me at my master's house ; he left about a quarter past 4 o'clock ; he told me he was going right off home ; he was then a little the worse for drink.

Mr. Taylor : From the appearance of the body and from the evidence as to the way in which he laid when found, I should say deceased died from suflocation ; I hear from the nurse that his hands were found clenched and were full of mud and leaves, showing that there was a struggle in the water ; he had no power to recover himself with his face or part of his face under water ; I have no doubt that suffocation was the cause of death

A Juryman : I don't think any one in the neighbour-hood is at all surprised.

Foreman : We were all aware of it. He had been a drunkard all his life.

Mr. Lee : Yes, for days together.

You can find the ditch on a globe at 0°43'36" Longitude, 51°56'47" Latitude. Or take the A604 from Halstead to Earls Colne, then second left to Countess Cross. Then take the right fork, then first right and round a bend. The second, sharper bend is Henry's corner.

Today, electric cables sizzle overhead and an oak has grown up on the spot. But the ditch is still three and a half feet deep with about three inches of water, still thick with brambles, holly, nettles, ivy, docks, thistle and wild roses. A sample of soil sent for analysis to the Hertfordshire College of Agriculture in a peanut butter jar revealed 15 times the normal lime.

I was not drunk, for I never mix alcohol with work. But as I lay there in that ditch I felt Henry's panic 109 years before flooding my body and I clawed in the black winter ditch and sucked for air to feel the shock of cold water in my mouth . . . And then blackness filled Henry's head.

Henry lay dead in that ditch four days! No one went to look for him. Maybe

such absences were not unusual. Or nobody cared.

Then on the following Saturday, James Sales, a cattle drover from Little Maplestead, was coming along the road between 12 and one o'clock midday when he "saw what appeared to be a greatcoat flung in the ditch and when I went up I saw it was the body of a man; he was lying on his face which was covered with water . . . I went back to Mrs Pilgrim's [at Great Catley's] and gave information, and afterwards helped to get the body out of the ditch." When they turned the body over, Henry was instantly recognised, even though his face was bruised and suffocated blue. His hands were clenched tight and full of mud and dead leaves, and, as PC Watts was later to observe, his shoe nails were quite rusted.

Henry's corpse was put on a cart and taken back to Pebmarsh that same day to lie in Esther's cottage while the village buzzed with scandal and hindsight. The following Monday morning the Pebmarsh establishment held an inquest at the Kings Head and by their proceedings opened a unique window into the life of this obscure Essex labourer. Henry was buried next day. I doubt Esther needed much consoling but I expect the genial Harbottle Grimston went through some appropriate motions, and no doubt looked up a suitable text for next Sunday's sermon.

Jemima Bush was 15. It was possibly the shock of her father's death which made her ill. The doctor diagnosed bronchitis, but Victorian diagnoses are notoriously slipshod and the background and course of her sickness make it almost certainly that most dreaded Victorian disease: TB.

Many doctors then simply (and wisely) prescribed food for such ailments. But this medicine was in short supply. Although some Pebmarsh labouring families grew their own vegetables and might keep a pig, in general their diet was very poor. And scandalously, as the historian Patricia Horn points out, "fresh milk was surprisingly scarce in rural areas – and especially at the end of the nineteenth century the situation became acute, as large quantities were dispatched by rail to the big urban centres, while skimmed milk was used to fatten the pigs".

Nor did the Pebmarsh climate help Jemima. Marshy Pebmarsh certainly is. More so before the recent draining and filling in. And old timers remember the brook flooding winters, drowning sheep and stranding fish in ditches. Jack Cook recalls one particular meadow where the Potter family kept pigs "until they drowned. 'Never mind,' said Mr Potter, 'I'll keep chickens, they can fly.'" But the chickens drowned too.

O Jemima minor. Her face took on the luminous stare of TB victims. She was racked with coughing, grew weaker and weaker. Then coughed blood. The doctor found an abcess – I expect on a lung, and probably prescribed opium to kill the pain. Her bed was put downstairs by the only fire in the poorly lit, damp, brick floored living room.

Esther worked at home plaiting straw and could gossip to Jemima as her fingers rapidly split, soaked and twisted the straw strips together. On washdays Esther boiled up a large copper and filled the room with the acrid tang of cheap soap and soda. Or she stirred cooking pots over the red spitting wood fire.

Jemima is propped up in bed, a cheap shawl hugged around her wasted shoulders. The cottage interior is so richly brown it vibrates with blue. Jemima's auburn hair spills carefully over rumpled pillows, done impasto ivory with pink tinted hollows. Her pallid face and scorching eyes are inclined longingly towards the translucent window panes and pale rays which silver the hopeless curves of her forearms and wrists.

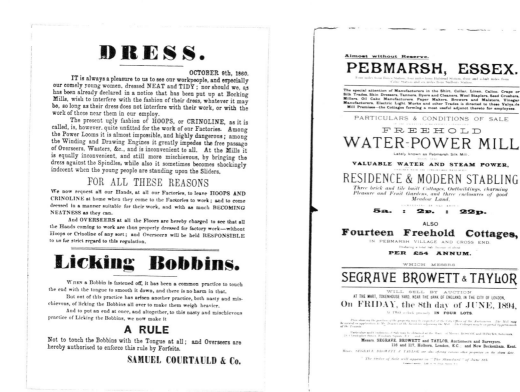

DRESS.

OCTOBER 9th, 1860.

IT is always a pleasure to us to see our workpeople, and especially our comely young women, dressed NEAT and TIDY; nor should we, as has been already declared in a notice that has been put up at Bocking Mills, wish to interfere with the fashion of their dress, whatever it may be, so long as their dress does not interfere with their work, or with the work of those near them in our employ.

The present ugly fashion of HOOPS, or CRINOLINE, as it is called, is, however, quite unfitted for the work of our Factories. Among the Power Looms it is almost impossible, and highly dangerous; among the Winding and Drawing Engines it greatly impedes the free passage of Overseers, Wasters, &c., and is inconvenient to all. At the Mills it is equally inconvenient, and still more mischievous, by bringing the dress against the Spindles, while also it sometimes becomes shockingly indecent when the young people are standing upon the Sliders.

FOR ALL THESE REASONS

We now request all our Hands, at all our Factories, to leave HOOPS AND CRINOLINE at home when they come to the Factories to work; and to come dressed in a manner suitable for their work, and with as much BECOMING NEATNESS as they can.

And OVERSEERS at all the Floors are hereby charged to see that all the Hands coming to work are thus properly dressed for factory work—without Hoops or Crinoline of any sort; and Overseers will be held RESPONSIBLE to us for strict regard to this regulation.

Licking Bobbins.

When a Bobbin is fastened off, it has been a common practice to touch the end with the tongue to smooth it down, and there is no harm in that.

But out of this practice has arisen another practice, both nasty and mischievous, of licking the Bobbins all over to make them weigh heavier.

And to put an end at once, and altogether, to this nasty and mischievous practice of Licking the Bobbins, we now make it

A RULE

Not to touch the Bobbins with the Tongue at all; and Overseers are hereby authorised to enforce this rule by Forfeits.

SAMUEL COURTAULD & Co.

Almost without Reserve.

PEBMARSH, ESSEX.

Four miles from Bures Station, four miles from Halstead Station, three and a half miles from Colne Station and six miles from Sudbury Station.

The special attention of Manufacturers in the Shirt, Collar, Linen, Calico, Crape or Silk Trades, Skin Dressers, Tanners, Dyers and Cleaners, Wool Staplers, Seed Crushers, Millers, Oil Cake Manufacturers, Paper Makers, Brewers and Maltsters, Vinegar Manufacturers, Electric Light Works and other Trades is directed to these Valuable Mill Premises—the Cottages forming a most useful adjunct thereto for employés.

PARTICULARS & CONDITIONS OF SALE

FREEHOLD
WATER-POWER MILL
Lately known as Pebmarsh Silk Mill.

VALUABLE WATER AND STEAM POWER,

RESIDENCE & MODERN STABLING
Three brick and tile built Cottages, Outbuildings, charming Pleasure and Fruit Gardens, and three enclosures of good Meadow Land,

5a. : 2r. : 22p.

ALSO

Fourteen Freehold Cottages,
IN PEBMARSH VILLAGE AND CROSS END.

Producing a total Sub Income of about

PER £54 ANNUM.

WHICH MESSRS

SEGRAVE BROWETT & TAYLOR
WILL SELL BY AUCTION
AT THE MART, TOKENHOUSE YARD, NEAR THE BANK OF ENGLAND, IN THE CITY OF LONDON,

On FRIDAY, the 8th day of JUNE, 1894,

At TWO o'clock precisely, IN FOUR LOTS.

Plans showing the property may be inspected at the City Offices of the Auctioneers. The Mill may be viewed on application to the Depositor of the Residence adjoining the Mill. The Cottages may be inspected by permission of the Tenants.

Particulars and Conditions of Sale may be obtained at the Mart; of Messrs. HOWCIE and HINCKS, Solicitors, 25 Christopher Street, Finsbury Square, E.C.;

116 and 117, Holborn, London, E.C. and New Beckenham, Kent.

Messrs. SEGRAVE, BROWETT and TAYLOR, Auctioneers and Surveyors,

Messrs. SEGRAVE, BROWETT & TAYLOR are also offering various other properties on the above date.

The Order of Sale will appear in "The Standard" of June 8th.

Left, a notice exhibited in one of the Courtauld silk mills in 1860; right, the Rodicks close the Pebmarsh Mill and prospects in the area dive.

The winter of 1874-5 snowed heavily. A thaw set in the first days of January with much flooding. In London, middle class children dressed up for New Year masques and fancy dress balls or went to cheer *Babes in the Wood* or *Aladdin* at Drury Lane. On January 5, 900 boy and girl orphans were treated to a late Christmas dinner at the boys' home in Great Queen Street. They feasted on roast beef and plum pudding and then sang "Scatter Ye Seeds of Kindness" "very prettily" for the Reverend R J Simpson. That same Tuesday dawned brighter than usual in Pebmarsh. The morning sun sparkled through clouds scudding south-west. And Jemima died.

But now begins our Bushes' long and eventually spectacular ascent.

In July 1877 Rachel Bush married James Robert Smith, a miller from the village of Bradwell. The 1881 Census tells us Esther Bush was living in a house with her son John 2, next door to her daughter Hannah Hicks, who was now widowed (William Hicks died at 34 of a chest disease) and lived with her two small children and 74 year old father-in-law.

Then on July 4 1882, John 2 married Martha Watkinson, a 19 year old native of Pebmarsh. They moved about two miles away to a (now demolished) cottage near Ashford Lodge in the village of Little Maplestead where on November 6 1886 Martha gave birth to Joseph Bush – Kate's grandfather.

In the 1880's England was slumped in agricultural depression. And prospects in the area fell further when in June 1882 the Rodicks suddenly gave their employees one month's notice and closed the Pebmarsh mill. (It never worked again and was demolished in 1901.) The straw plaiting industry also crashed and by 1891 was "practically extinct". The population of Little Maplestead fell from 407 in 1841 to 261 in 1881. By 1901 only 193 were left.

Many migrated to London or its outskirts. John and Martha joined them. In 1901 we find them 40 miles away in a "dwelling house" in Grange Lane in the south Essex village of South Ockenden. John, obviously an able and trusted worker, is a farm foreman. They settled in South Ockenden for good. Which is the setting of our next Bush drama.

V

A grinning Tommy in a trench, dirt showers over advancing troops, the Kaiser canters by. . . A suitably flickering and grainy grey past – speeded up for antique effect and dubbed with cheering, bangs and clip clop. The Great War. Visual anecdotes to front a factory of death whose well oiled wheels unrolled 6,000 corpses every day – for 1,500 days. And by 1916 so many had been killed that conscription was enacted to prolong the slaughter.

But conscription produced an outburst of revulsion. And a movement of conscientious objection organised with a speed, ingenuity and courage which makes our CND seem juvenile. The Government hastily set up local "tribunals" of worthies to assess the sincerity (as they put it) of each conscientious objector. (These tribunals also decided which occupations were of sufficient "national importance" for exemption.)

"What going before the tribunal means in essence," wrote one CO: "is 'Go before Mr G____.' See him – not as a customer in his shop when he is anxious to oblige you, not on the friendly footing of a business equal, not in any of the open-hearted intimacies of his private life – see him on a tribunal. See him seated at a table in the public view, dressed in a little brief authority and accompanied by all the petty pomp and circumstance with which borough officials freeze human souls. Explain to him what it is almost impossible for any human being to explain. Satisfy him about something which he entirely fails to understand. Answer every silly question, put up with every foolish gibe. If Mr G____ will exempt you, that will be sufficient. If he refuses, you will be seized upon and ground up inside the military machine."

(J Scott Duckers, Handed Over)

Army officers prosecuted at these mock trials and went for their victims with relish. The *Romford Times* for 1917 immortalises one Lieutenant Percy

Weston: "Mr G Berridge, secretary of the Gas Company, said Mr Earthy's work was very important, and it took a long time to get a thorough grasp of it. Lieutenant Weston: I am going to press for this man, and I am going to have him if I can get him." Of Archibald George Rich, a 40 year old widower with six children, Lieutenant Weston said "he thought it would be much better for Mr Rich and his children if Mr Rich went into the army."

There was a barely suppressed hysteria about these proceedings – "outbursts" of laughter, "witty remarks" at the CO's expense, and tirades:

"He cannot claim to be a socialist *and* a conscientious objector."

Chairman to CO: "Have you read where He went into the temple with a whip and lashed them out?" CO: "But He did not kill them." Chairman: "No but He probably would have done if He had had a gun."

CO: "Jesus said ye cannot serve two masters." Chairman: "But I say you *can* serve two masters!"

To a CO: "You are nothing but a shivering mass of unwholesome fat!"

"You ought to be hanged. You ought to be shot."

"There are two things you possess – cowardice and insolence."

"You are qualifying for a lunatic asylum."

"You are a traitor and only fit to be on the point of a German bayonet."

"This man . . . is a scandalous disgrace to the parish."

Equally fantastic were the remarks made to a South Ockenden slaughterhouse man. The chairman declared he found this CO's views incompatible with his occupation and a Mr E T Snelling remarked that "so far as he could hear [sic] there was no difference between killing Germans and killing pigs". They refused him exemption. He was Joseph Bush, Kate's grandfather.

Despite Mr Snelling's reservations, Joe Bush had thought long and hard about his objections to war. He was a most thoughtful man who moved between the Pentecostalists, in the town of Grays, and the South Ockenden Weslyans.

Mrs Bailey, a Pentecostalist, recalls Joe: "I used to love his ministry. He was so cool, calm and collected. He knew what he was talking about . . . poor old Joe." ["Why do you say poor old Joe?"] "Just a term . . . I was thinking to myself about the way he used to walk and persevere and plod on, you know. It was a time of plodding. These days they all want it laid on for them. . ."

Joe also read the Bible evenings in the Wesleyan Chapel with Mr Cook and Mr Christmas. They were St John's Ambulancemen and when war came joined the RAMC to avoid killing. But Joe hesitated. And then it was too late.

Joe appealed to the higher County Tribunal but was turned down. It seems he now had a failure of nerve for he reappeared at the Local Tribunal in June 1916 asking for his case to be reopened and declaring that while he still couldn't fight he was prepared to do "work of national importance". Dismissed.

Being a CO at the height of jingoistic mania in 1916 was a lonely, unpopular and courageous stand. And uncharted ground in terms of possible consequences. Joe was frequently taunted by local patriots with cries of "conchi! conchi!". And "they used to hit the door," Mr Cook's brother told us, "stone the door." Eventually Joe was arrested and within a month was imprisoned in Wormwood Scrubs – known in those days as the "spiritual headquarters" of the CO movement.

But by now the Government, having locked up thousands of principled and frequently outstanding men, was highly embarrassed by the CO question. (There were altogether about 16,000 COs and more than 6,000 were imprisoned at least once.) The flavour of this new "criminal class" is vividly conveyed in an autobiography:

"A religious service of some kind was in progress at almost every hour of every working day; and as the members of each denomination had, at the given moment, to be marshalled together from the various halls, exercise-yards and workshops, and as prisoners were in all their movements escorted by officers, a vast and intricate organisation was involved, which obviously irked some of the warders who were not themselves spiritually-minded. Never shall I forget the tones, now wearily resigned, now crisply mordant, in which the chief warder of my hall punctuated the daily round with cries of 'Send down the Roman Catholics'; or 'Send down the Baptists'; for 'Send down the Peculiars'! He had a true histrionic gift, and I think he relished his own performances, especially when, like a prophet invoking an expected miracle, he shouted jubilantly: 'SEND DOWN THE CHURCH OF CHRIST.' "

(Gilbert Thomas, *Autobiography*)

Eventually it was decided to set up a Central Tribunal to review CO cases and offer work of "national importance" instead of prison. Appointed to head this important body was Edward Hubert Gascoigne-Cecil, Fourth Marquis of Salisbury, an Old Etonian and Tory bigwig. The prisoners "were brought, weakened and exhausted, from their cells, in total ignorance of what was before them, to a tribunal within prison walls, and in the prison atmosphere. The proceedings were of the briefest; apparently about three minutes to each was usual." Joe was interrogated during the afternoon of the 10th of August, case number 216.

So here is Joe Bush, 30 years old, a shortish man, taciturn and shy. He faces a large table scattered with ominous looking papers behind which sits the

formidable Lord Salisbury. Next to Salisbury is the bristling Scots million-
aire, Sir George Younger, Chairman of Youngers Brewery (and Joe a
teetotaller!). And on either side two lesser gentlemen.

```
                     CENTRAL  TRIBUNAL
                ─────────────────────────

        One hundred & twenty-eighth meeting 10th August 1916
                ─────────────────────────

        Present:- Lord Salisbury, Sir George Younger, Mr. Brunner &
                  Mr. Agg Gardner.


(1)     The following cases were decided at Wormwood Scrubs Prison:-

        No              Name                        Decision

W    92            J.C.Coles                        A
"    91            J.A.Trustram                     "
"    90            G.Perrin                         "
"   279            A. Wild                          "
"   216            J. Bush                          "
```

What can Joe tell these people in three minutes about his prayers, his study
of the Bible, his discussions with friends and ideas about charity and Christian
duty? But something about Joe impressed them, they accepted his sincerity
and offered him alternative work.

> "Those given outdoor work - timber cutting, road making, quarrying, railway
> maintenance and agriculture - were housed under canvas or in huts. Those on
> indoor work - mailbag, brush and basket making - were. . . housed in prisons,
> workhouses and asylums. All were subject to police surveillance and paid
> through the police. In short, they were. . . treated as political prisoners. . ."
>
> (David Boulton, *Objection Overruled*)

And COs were frequently insulted and physically attacked. (About 70
actually died from mistreatment.)

So Joe passed the war to end all wars. So "Joseph Bush" isn't just one of 44
dead names carved in black on the little war memorial on South Ockenden
Green (what a toll for this small village!).* And Joe eventually fathered a
doctor who fathered Kate Bush who between them, I think, have done more
for the country *I* live in than the energetic Salisbury with his six pages in the
Dictionary of National Biography.

---

*And it seems both Joe's pacifist friends who joined the RAMC were killed! Charlie Cook still
mourns his brother Harold, "the brightest of the family", buried over 65 years ago in a mass grave
in France.

VI

Today South Ockenden is an ugly municipal shanty town of maisonettes and garages with a prefabricated social centre, sprawling south from the old village church, pub and green. But in those days, says Violet Blows, "Ockenden was Ockenden people, one big family". It was famous in the area for its red brick Wesleyan chapel to which labourers walked from miles around.

This was the chapel frequented by Joe Bush. But Joe's thoughts had sometimes strayed from God. To one of the organists. A light redhead with swept-back hair, a bright manner and persuasive alto singing voice. And with the lovely name of Annie May Carder.

Annie lived with her father, John Carder, a village character and noted daredevil who "would race up tall ladders without thinking". John was a labourer who also cut the villagers' hair ("pudding bowl style") and "he was a doorkeeper in the Wesleyan. And he used to sit in the back seat, about three down, and he'd sit holding a hard sweet in his mouth. And the old chap used to doze off [*laughs*] and it would choke him."

Annie and Joe married on August 2 1919 and moved into John Carder's home at 6 North Road, a tiny two storey house squeezed between the general store and village post office. On April 4 1920 Robert John Bush, Kate's father, was born.

South Ockenden was a close place then. The station master knew all his commuters and held up trains for latecomers. Nurse Scott cycled around the village dispensing stern kindness. Three pubs! And when old Jack Michelberger had a drop too much he'd stand at his gate shouting in his German accent and swinging a cane at passers-by. The two Hasler sisters kept the local post office with a sideline in wool and anyone wanting to phone after hours just "knocked them up". "It was a book! It was a book!" says Violet Blows.

Queenie Rainbird also recently recalled those days for a local history magazine. She had lived next door to and was a friend of Kate's father (known as Jack or Jackie):

"There were just the three buildings in the row and opposite were the dairy and the saddler's shop. Jackie, seven years old to my six, was a year younger than Mary. He used to deliver telegrams for Miss Hasler, the postmistress. He

Left: In this tiny house (smarter then), Annie May Carder was born, brought up, lived with her husband Joseph Bush, gave birth to and raised Kate's father, and died. Right: Inside the South Ockenden Wesleyan Chapel where Joe and Annie fell in love.

had an upright, yellow bike which he rode as if the Devil was after him. Jackie would say, 'Got half-a-crown today. Took me an hour and a half, though. Right the other side of Bulvan fen.' We envied Jackie."

Joe was now a milkman, collecting milk in churns from farms and delivering around the village on a horse and cart. Then he became a delivery man for the Salmon family's hardware business – a job he kept for the rest of his working life. He drove around in a Ford van stacked with goods and delivered paraffin door to door.

Joe and Annie were a quiet and aloof couple, remembered with affection. Joe's implacability was a legend: "You know, some people would say perhaps: 'I'd like to put a squib behind him.' "

Sunday mornings they set of punctually for the Wesleyan just around the corner – Joe smart in a bowler hat and carrying a big black Bible. They were a steadying influence at the chapel where discussions could drag and tempers sometimes flared over fine points of scripture and organisation. Services were lively with shouts of "praise the Lord, brother!", and some sermons disputed with, "no brother! no brother!". The chapel was also a social centre with mothers' meetings, a young men's fellowship, concerts and a Sunday school. Joe eventually became a member of the chapel committee, and Annie was often on her knees scrubbing the chapel floor spotless. Joe and Annie also held prayer meetings in their house: "a hymn and then a prayer and then perhaps a little chat and someone would probably give a little talk on some scripture". And Joe preached on the village green, with Annie singing and playing a fold-up portable organ and people sitting around on the grass. . .

And here discretion draws a veil. There is plenty more to tell of those interesting times but some of its people are still alive and may want to tell their own stories. So I'll précis the events leading up to Kate's birth on July 30 1958 and then tell the suburban adventure which puts the final touches to her story.

South Ockendon, The Green and Church.

South Ockendon, South Road.

Kate's father was an exceptionally determined student who won a scholarship to Grays grammar school and went on to medical school. He graduated in 1943 and married Hannah Daly, a staff nurse at Long Grove Hospital in Epsom, three years his senior (as Annie was Joe's) and an Irish farmer's daughter. Dr. Bush became a GP in Bexley and then Welling. Annie died in 1950 and Joe moved into his son's spacious new home – the 350 year old East Wickham Farmhouse. Joe was 72 when Hannah gave birth to Kate. And Kate was five when Joe died at the farmhouse in the freezing winter of '63.

It's nice to think the old conchi held Kate Bush in his arms.

VII

Pop is the only art which really counts today. Our most progressive – responsive, mutable, hungry and eclectic – form. The taskmaster and pacemaker of all the arts. It stands now where painting stood in the early century, as the focus of problems and innovation: our leader art.

Meanwhile the avant garde has turned itself into a display of fossilised passions and polemic as dignified and predictable as classical ballet. And no more important. A show put on for a public of bankers, civil servants and TV producers interested merely in investment potential – for securities or reputations. Hardly art at all, since it no longer moves, surprises or alerts us. Merely mystifies, bores or impresses. This avant garde boldly announces its allegiance to Eternal Values and sneers at hit parades. But forgets what the old modernists knew very well. That only *contingent* art interests future generations: art grounded in and fraught with the moment, art rooted in ephemera, in love with the detail and the people (not an idea) of history. As Simone de Beauvoir pointed out, no one now bothers with Rousseau's laboured "masterpiece", *Les rêveries du promeneur solitaire*. Or can ignore his *Confessions*.

But states and bureaucrats love dead art and fear the risk, excitement and danger of living art. So just as the Soviet Union mounts its Bolshoi under Czarist chandeliers, the British Arts Council mounts a symposium on John Cage. Yet who will remember John Cage in 100 years? Or not know Kate Bush?

But pop is also a new and uncertain art. An art which uniquely encompasses music, performance, publicity, image, fetish. Which oscillates between public and private obsessions, polarises (so makes a crisis of) fame and anonymity, power and impotence. And an art continually boiling over into life: shattering categories and limits, frothing along the interface of belief and activity – continually exploding dreams into reality: promising the earth!

Our ideas about pop are dim indeed. For our thinkers prefer theses on Lalo to Lennon, Pierrot Lunaire to Phil Spector, Kate Greenaway to Kate Bush. So we have to rely on teleological terms like "commercial", "photogenic", "production", "image" – without realising the large questions these terms imply.

Pop in fact is the Romantic movement of our consumer civilisation. And just as the Romantics put heaven and hell on earth by imagining the fantastic social and personal possibilities opened by the unprecedented power and creativity of the first Industrial Revolution, so pop's impetus and imagination comes from its projection of the second, electrical, petro-chemical and consumer-based industrial revolution, which began at the turn of this century and became especially apparent from the twenties. Dada (which is where pop really begins), jazz, Surrealism and rock'n'roll pro-claimed the riot of "lifestyles": the manifesto of consumerism, which shook, shocked, blasted and *rocked* away the anti-consumerist opposition. A relent-less, global tattoo, conscripting and drilling millions into a previously avant garde modernism.

But Romanticism also locked the social potential of the Industrial Revolution inside the prison yard of Art. It imagined desire through idealist philosophical shapes: as wishfulness, sublimation, fantasy – dreams. Dreams which nevertheless continually threatened to escape, to burst through "genius" and "revolution".

So the characteristic tension of a Romantic work, its violent beauty and beautiful violence, its passionate images as images of passion, its frustration and crisis of form, is its perpetual *tumescence*: it always seems on the edge of itself; about to break into life, realise its promise.

As indeed it does in those exotic Romantic borders (or Romantic sub-systems) where life becomes art and vice versa. In pornography, sentimen-tality and revolutionary rhetoric. Where all the dizziness of Art as behaviour, Expression as self-expression, is realised. Napoleon crowns himself, the Sadeian tortures a child, Chopin coughs blood over his keyboard, Blanqui lights a fuse, Florence Nightingale lights a lamp, Jack the Ripper operates on a whore, and Zola's Claude Lantier paints a yet more outrageous canvas...

Likewise pop promises to "spring" the consumer revolution, to break the mould of art and let its anarchistic spirit run riot in history. For pop is very much, and increasingly, the "art of behaviour". And concentrates an anxiety which haunts most of our art one way or the other: that the centre might succumb to its edges: imagination enact its utopias and nightmares.

And pop is also the principal theatre of that major consumerist invention: everyday life. It charges mundanity: ordinary people, voices, gestures, pretensions with mystic grandeur. A *missa cantata* for love's broken promises or the leader of the pack. Its hits are black whirlpools of affectivity, luminous moments which lift ordinary lives to transcendence, bathe dullness with rhapsodic purpose, texture our intimacies and punctuate memories – touch us all with History. The music not of the spheres but of the quotidian – that artistic space blown open by Joyce's *Ulysses*.

And the only art fully integrated with mass media. So pop artists must project their work through celebrity games and pin-ups as much as music. Not all of them understand this clearly or can sustain the difficulties. Some recoil after a while from limelight thinking it an unwanted and unnecessary burden on their simple craft, protesting they are only performers who once tripped a wire and set a madhouse going. . . And then become inconsolable when they lose their touch, their "appeal". For are they not the same people as before, just as talented, and possibly even harder working? And writing much better songs?. . .

Around here some tricky problems begin. Kate Bush says, for instance, that "only her work counts". She protests at the intrusions and demands of journalists and tries to run her career like a corner sweet shop. I'd like to say good luck to her. And a pound of gobstoppers! Only isn't part of her work to be famous? Because a pop artist's art is to project a personality as much as a melody, live out and *embody* fantasies, to sell habits, quirks and lifestyles as much as ideas. Much more so than in any other art. And it's Kate's fortune, or misfortune, to be one of those very rare "naturals" for this hybrid and ambivalent art. She's a classic pop artist: a voice/name/sound/face/image/expression/personality/biography all woven into so unique a style no one can imitate (no one even covers her songs) or ignore her. Tailor-made for the media, a bonanza for curiosity. And with more camera presence than any actress of her generation (and all the film industry can offer her is remakes of *A Star is Born*).

A pop star is a celebrity *par excellence*. And as that wise American sociologist who spent his life investigating the mysteries of celebrity, Orrin E Klapp, wrote:

"[The] feeling of being public property is not an illusion; it reflects the truth that the public has adopted the celebrity as an image of a certain kind and expects him to perform the functions of that image. He is no longer just a person but has become an institution. Since he is 'our' Will, 'our' George, 'our' John, the public assumes the right to criticize, guide, and make demands. Celebrities often complain of requests made of them by strangers, who ask for loans, gifts, or advice or claim relationship of one kind or another. The status of celebrity as public property also helps explain intrusions on his privacy, familiarities by strangers, people who crowd into photographs with him, and even the curious 'touching mania'. The Duke of Windsor remarked that while he was Prince of Wales, people used to try to touch him by any means, prod him, even hit him with folded newspapers."

(Symbolic Leaders)

So has Kate complained about being stared at and touched by strangers. But the starers and touchers *doubt she exists*. Her appearance is like a Hoover vacuum cleaner coming to life. No wonder they're fascinated. But can she really excite curiosity and then hide? Or put her subjectivity on the market and then complain of lack of privacy? I'm not sure.

But I do think there's a political problem involved.

For the star exercises power without responsibility. Is not accountable for his or her influence. Which is dangerous. So journalists and commentators see it their job to scale down, open up, criticise and even ridicule stars.

Extremely naive is the pop star's familiar complaint of being traduced, misrepresented, etc, by the press. They certainly are. But so what? Why should *what* they say be important? Pop stars are not interviewed for truth or wisdom, but to produce newspaper copy. To tell stories. Most star interviews are simply presence fetishes. And it hardly matters what David Bowie or Adam Ant have to say about the numerous things they know very little about. If they have anything to say it will be in their work. Otherwise they might leave philosophy to philosophers. Who in return promise not to sing and dance.

Even so, I still don't know. I wrote the first biography of Kate Bush with my wife, Judy. It turned into an anti-star book which we felt was needed then. I deliberately inverted the stock form and content and exaggerated the clichés and tricks of pop biography and journalism to the point of lunacy

Top, Bali exorcist dance; bottom left, reaching for Pope John Paul II; bottom right, Kate at a fan club convention.

where I thought they might become transparent. But many read it "straight" as an exposé/attack on Kate (and entourage) rather than on what she represented – or a comment on *how* she was represented. Moreover Kate's no Toyah Willcox and was quite hurt. Justifiably, for I'd forgotten the person and pursued my logic without regard to her feelings – and even without coming clean with myself about how much I admired her work, since this would have slowed me down and spoilt my fun. The critic made the writer dishonest. I should have recalled a scathing passage that most gentle of writers, Gaston Bachelard, has about critics:

"The phenomenologist has nothing in common with the literary critic who, as has frequently been noted, judges a work that he could not create and, if we are to believe certain facile condemnations, would not want to create. A literary critic is a reader who is necessarily severe. By turning inside out like a glove an overworked complex that has become debased to the point of being part of the vocabulary of statesmen, we might say that the literary critic and the professor of rhetoric, who know-all and judge-all, readily go in for a simplex of superiority."

(The Poetics of Space)

Desire and distance, intimacy and exclusion are the paradox and tension of the star's art. His or her *raison d'etre* is to come close, make us care, to fire our curiosity, come into our living rooms, walk into our bedrooms, slip inside our dreams. But the "bigger", hence more "real", the star is, the more remote.

With what impertinence do some stars complain about fans. After all the fan may legitimately *demand* a share of attention. May even ask: "Since you fill me, why should I not claim you?" EMI and I am you. My God, where will it all end?

We are now close to those dark places where Hinckley stalked Jodie Foster and Chapman waited for Lennon. Where the gruesome culture of autograph hunters turns mad.

But the fan haunted by a star, who assumes the star's identity, then seeks out the star's flesh to possess, or even kill the star, is really only working out a transformation *invited* by pop. Which is an apt, even an elegant, formulation of its logic. Only a fool or the *New Musical Express* would imagine (as they did and ran the "story" for three issues) a CIA plot when it is the industry the *NME* serves, its own logic, the moods it exists to create which "brainwashed" – as they quaintly put it – and "directed" Chapman to his sordid apotheosis. What a blind panic of bad faith must reign in Carnaby Street!

The same bad faith with which *The Fan*, a Hollywood movie, ascribed a fan's murderous frenzy solely to his psychosis. Without even mentioning Hollywood's *systematic art* of incitement: its art of arousing longing, envy and resentment – a more important and conspicuous Hollywood art, after all, than acting.

Only the coda is missing. But that will come. Some record company will sign one of these killers up. And the record will be a hit! You think I joke, but wait – a dialectic, the movement of ideas to their crisis, nearly always overwhelms its actors.

We do have institutions, of course, to prevent such horrors. Fan clubs, for example. Which control and contain, and also rather desperately try to jollify and trivialise the fan's fanaticism. So they solemnly elect presidents and treasurers, hold meetings, debate the authenticity of mementoes, mail out newsletters, trade honestly in relics, and supplicate "appearances".

Even so there is no thinking so consistently fantastic, no emotional tone as hot or rhetoric so manic as the pop fan's. To find a parallel for their odd mixture of calculation and hysteria, their volatility and wishful exegesis, you have to go back to Christianity's most opaque and feverish moment: to medieval religious hagiography: to the cult of saints, martyrs, miracles and relics.

Only here, in, say, Gregory of Tours' amazingly tall and passionately fulsome tales of hazardous pilgrimages, tortured portents and visions, decipherings and transformations and violent miracles, will you find anything approaching our fanzines, fanscreams and fandreams.

Because for all the press gushes about sexy Kate Bush and even while girls throw knickers at Mick Jagger's lips and themselves at Billy Idol, the carefully exaggerated and heightened and devotional *tone* of this sexuality, its idealism, is clearly a metaphor for something else. As is the self-immolation of groupies. A mystical wisdom. For just as the nun by her symbolic marriage to Christ achieves a sublime tension of impossible consummation and sets us all an example, so the fan's symbolic intimacy with a star demonstrates a quasi-religious ecstasy of longing and belonging. The fan is a spiritual hero, the *perfect consumer*, who shows us how to have our cake and eat it.

We all want transcendence. To be filled, haunted, possessed by a supernatural presence. To be intimate with Greatness: saved from anonymity. So we baptise, even drown ourselves, in the star's holy charisma – that golden aura which is a legend of our own humdrum roles, our self-regard magically "produced" and re-produced. The pop star is a miracle of banality.

"... the people devotedly went to the cell of the blessed man in which he often had lingered in converse with angels. They licked each place with their kisses, or wet with their tears each place where the blessed man had sat, or had prayed, or where he had taken food, or where he had granted sleep to his body after many labors."

(Gregory of Tours. Sixth century AD)

I remember that first EMI poster which loomed from buses and tube stations to katenap my eye in '78. Grave, delicious Kate, plump owl in her

tangled nest of puzzled hair with nipples blowing tiny kisses through a cotton vest. Kate and I joined in instant photolock. Kate Bush, bushy Kate laid out for me by the EMI artroom boys with a gourmet's delight like a table for guests. A strawberry tea spread, with eyes like doughnuts full of jam, and butter lips and full cream cheeks spread with a blunt knife by the vicar's wife...

So I turn Kate's glossy pages, crackling and soapy to the touch, paper which seems limp and heavy and wet with *realism*, as if her images were oozing and perspiring into my fascinated inspection. Where she opens herself ultra-bright and ultra-sharp with what seems like almost effusive precision. A kind of alacrity. An implacably sunny and heartlessly optimistic photoworld where I can dwell for ever and ever with no problem or effort, and no hope of change or decay, over her lambent skin and sticky promise of her tropical lips.

Kate Bush is our goddess Frig. And like the Saxons we both revere *and* fear her. Shroud her in the mystery of her power and the power of her mystery.

A fertility goddess for our Nature: the Economy. Mother Commodity.

Kate Bush is the smile on the steel of EMI, the mating call of Thorn Industries, British capital on heat, the soft warm voice of mass media, the sweet breath of vinyl, the lovely face of bureaucracy, the seductive gaze of power. As every star is.

And she also incarnates pure adventure, total freedom: the ad made flesh. Fabulously rich, we rumour: an idol in our world-wide superstitious cult of celebrity, which is the only religion we all truly believe in now – even a pope has to be a celebrity before we take him seriously. The negative image of ourselves. Of our anonymity and powerlessness. Which her images dramatise and expiate. Kate Catharsis.

No wonder EMI takes such care to show her with the same scrupulous art as Moscow depicts Karl Marx and Thorn Industries its computers. Through hybrid images which hover just between photography and painting – pictures which exist just beyond the camera's conventional vision but retain a ghostly residue of its authority. The art of airbrush and stencil , soft pencil and rubber. The visual style proper to charismatic icons: celebrities are shown with its anonymous clarity, with the hard lustre of machinery and apotheosis. They appear to *shine*, by virtue of apparently effortless and bland tonal transitions, sharp black and white highlights, and meticulously separated edges – detail given with hypnotic brilliance which displays people as if they had suddenly loomed, ready-made and perfect, like smooth obelisks from a fog into which they might also disappear – monumental and intangible.

But I like her so much because she also spoils it for them. She has Monroe's flawed and flagrant presence. No wet-shine, deep-frozen cover-girl. No Beauty. Not Debbie Harry's vacuous nonentity – no blank screen for wet consumer dreams. But a woman who besides posing looks like she might menstruate, or sign cheques – or punch my nose. A self-contained exuberance which cheerfully stains the most pompous male tableau with female energy and wit.

And her favourite photolook is the gaze openly returned to a friend. Intimate, but not for sale.

VIII

"In my dome of ivory, a home of activity"
(Kate Bush: "Sat in Your Lap")

She reminds me very much of Raoul Dufy*, the "painter of all things tender", with his radiant blue spaces and brushwork as alarmingly fragile as her voice is.

And as with Dufy there's also something very healing about her work. A rare ability to be joyful and courage to be transparent. Judy Vermorel played it to the composer John Taverner, who'd never heard it before (he usually lives hermit-like in Greece). Taverner remarked at once and enthusiastically how unusually "beautiful" it was. Beautiful and peaceable. When the easier option, as Taverner also pointed out, is to exploit ugliness and stress.

Some of this comes from her family tradition – a resolute flight from violence over at least three generations. From Joe Bush's stand to Dr and Hannah Bush's career of medicine. Then their remarkably sane and open-handed raising of Kate and elder brothers, Jay and Paddy. An upbringing without time-killing, dream-wasting sado-masochistic rituals. Which gave Kate enough time, space and attention to dream freely and is certainly at the root of her creativity. Her brothers followed this tradition through their own

*Also of David Hockney who shares her lightness of touch, eclectic wit and suburban instinct. But what's revealing is the variation in the levels of quality and the volume of both these artists' output. Because Hockney can follow Picasso's sage advice: "not every painting has to be a masterpiece". He can show us a pencil sketch, a polaroid, a litho, or a canvas. But pop artists are constrained by the politics and economics of their record companies (and also a little by their own greed) to only put out possible "masterpieces". Finished Works. Which is very limiting to an artist's trial and error and feeling for a public.

[67]

art and also through Karate, a most dramatic way to contain and channel aggression, which philosophically, of course, is pacifistic. And Kate's own self-control and dislike of aggression is legendary.*

*I think she can't *understand* anger. Doesn't know what it is. She's recalled of her schooldays that: ". . . there were people who picked on me and gave me a very hard time. I was very thin and younger than most in my class so I was rather like the runt of the litter. I'd get hit occasionally. . . And I never fought back. I was aware of a lot of my friends being into things that I wasn't into. Like sarcasm. It had never been a part of my family – they still don't use sarcasm." And make-up artist Kirsty Climo told Judy Vermorel: "Her capability is remarkable, the way she copes with people pressing against her and questioning her. I've seen her in situations which I would have found intolerable. She almost has an ethereal quality about her. And gives out calmness to the people around her." Which is a large part of what attracts people to her work. I've never known such wide and deep loyalty to a pop star. And many of these admirers never even buy her records. One middle-aged man in a photo-library once tore up a photo I'd dug up of her looking gloriously drunk and holding a champagne glass. Also, she thinks that avuncular hippy Captain Beefheart was a proto-punk. What would she have made of Sid Vicious?! In fact one of the greatest compliments ever paid to her must be Malcolm McLaren's after the only occasion he met her, so he said, in EMI. Apparently she remarked on the "bad vibes" in the room and left immediately. And as McLaren rasped to me later, "Christ, man, she really looks *horrific*!" So I know exactly how *good* she looked from this man then at the apex of his career of systematic negativity and spite. His report of their encounter started to make me see through McLaren's creative pretensions and also made me think about my own career and attitudes – and in the end I found I had to publicly denounce McLaren (to the embarrassment of some EMI figures) and take the Bush camp more seriously and sympathetically. Despite her occasional arrogance and a rather rigid closed shop attitude to her work, aggression is beyond her. I'm not sure it that's right, or feasible, in such a wicked world. But it's very attractive.

"I think losing your temper is a waste of time and a bloody nuisance. If you're uptight about something it's often your own fault so you should keep it to yourself. If someone does something that I'm really not into, if they're doing something to offend me or someone I love then I will assume annoyance to get at them but I don't really mean it." (Kate Bush)

An attitude she also had as a child.

"Kate had like a sort of Wendy house at the bottom of the garden they built for her when she was little, done out properly – little table and chairs and such. And it was slightly off the ground and Took [a pet rabbit] used to go and run underneath it and then come out. One night it was getting quite late so Kate's mum said you had better bring him in. So we went out there and Kate had the brilliant idea of jumping on the floor inside so that he would come out: he would be frightened and come out. And we were both gaily jumping along when Took jumped out and jumped on the floor and I trod on him and broke his leg. We had to take him to the vet. I didn't go over for a couple of weeks because I felt so guilty, I felt awful. But nobody said anything to me about that. I thought they would all explode and say you stupid child, because I'm sure that's what I would have said. But nobody said a damn thing. Kate sort of picked him up and took him down to the vet. Rather than explode in your face she wouldn't say anything. I think she was the sort of person who wouldn't hurt your feelings if she didn't have to." (Diane Carman, old schoolfriend)

You could easily misjudge them. As I did once. Ascribing Kate's placid temperament to drugs and Gurdjieffian rituals. Maligning Jay Bush's introspection as sinister. And, most stupidly of all, I took the family's closeness for the jealousy of a joint stock company. I wasn't alone in this and took my cue from others. Strange rumours of cabals and exotic plots occasionally sweep the acrilan corridors of EMI and *NME*. Some people are still throwing (metaphorical) stones at the Bushes' front door. But there are no devils inside. Only a lesson.

The other key to her work is suburbia. She is profoundly suburban, acutely tuned to its everyday poetry and found bricolage: knee high brick walls turreted like castles, pink and fawn stucco, pavements cracked with grass, or Fanny on the Hill, the common behind her childhood home, littered with burnt mattresses, dwarf trees and Wonderloaf wrappings, behind which rise the green hills and white stones of Plumstead Cemetery and, beyond that, Bostall Woods where she could picnic or let the dog run up and down wooded gullies – ten miles from Charing Cross.

She has the suburban's deep emotion of home: the sense of dwelling and belonging. She would agree with Bachelard: "If I were asked to name the chief benefit of the house, I should say: the house shelters daydreaming, and the house protects the dreamer, the house allows one to dream in peace."

Suburbs were invented to mass produce such dreaming. A revolution as important, possibly more important, than the bold declarations of the French Revolution. And a frontier more exciting than the American West. For suburbia is humanity's *new* frontier: a global setting, stable yet elastic enough to accommodate and extend every kind of attitude, passion and hobby, expertise and madness. Where a devout Buddhist can live in the same street as a woodwork freak, a leather fetishist and a Brahms expert. A truly anarchistic society: pluralistic, cosmopolitan, diverse and inquisitive.

Kate inside East Wickham Farmhouse poses for Barry Plummer on the family's lionskin rug.

And suburbans are the most sensuous people in history.

They cultivate intimacies and sensations with an elaboration which to others may seem exotic, if not perverse. They have evolved, and continue to refine through their experimental culture of luxury, the most subtle and evanescent pleasures of inhabiting, owning and relationship. Suburban homes are planned, furnished and decorated to elicit the most delicate plays

An art between the suburban sentimentality of Victorian genre and Dufy's incisive and deft joie de vivre. Top, F G Cotman, "One of the Family" (Walker Art Gallery, Liverpool); bottom, Raoul Dufy, "Circus Horses" (private collection).

of atmosphere and nuances of proximity, privacy, meeting and drama. And to blur the gradations of sleeping and wakefulness with as many occasions as possible for the body to float, rock, recline, sink and encounter things which are already rounded, smooth, polished, coated. . . So the home becomes a symbolic body, the first body a child knows after his parents'.

And suburbans mark their children's memories with sensuous rituals as deep and lasting as the facial scars of some African tribes. Richard Church mentions a key one in his suburban autobiography:

The East Wickham Farmhouse in its wildly overgrown garden, a rustic sprawl in the heart of inch pinching suburbia. "I thought whatever are we entering into!" "It was really creepy, a strange place." And allegedly haunted by a Victorian serving maid.

"...the wonderful Sunday...morning hour when I crept into bed beside her [his mother], to fondle her there, to murmur to her in a kind of Garden of Eden bliss, and to feel her gentle response so acutely that I could hardly bear the joyous pain of it, and had to turn away...on these occasions Father was lying on the other side of her, and probably Jack [his elder bother] would be there too, all four of us squeezed into the great six-poster bed, indulgent and relaxed at the beginning of the Day of Rest."

(Over the Bridge)

The size of East Wickham Farm made Kate's home a social centre for her friends. Its front is almost concealed by large trees and a lushly overgrown garden while the back gives on to common land (where ponies are kept by a local club) and distant views of wooded hills. The house sprawls under a complicated huddle of roofs and white chimneys and spreads into several outbuildings including an old barn. Here Jay Bush had painted "the devil's mouth" and his poetry over the walls. In the barn loft illuminated by a small

oval window Kate and friends would smoke illicitly and "listen to Dave Edmunds records". The barn also housed an organ which Kate played until "it literally fell apart", gnawed away by mice. In the back garden was a swimming pool round which Kate and brothers sometimes held parties.

Inside the house Hannah Bush had created a highly polished and plush interior, enhancing the rich atmosphere of dreamlike angles and levels and creaking stairs and corridors and the subtle moods and plays of light which fill the house with peace.

Dr Bush was a genial, balding man with gingerish side whiskers, a low key manner and exceedingly sharp eyes. (He retains strong elements of an Essex country accent – as does Kate, especially when singing.) He is most characteristically remembered evenings, puffing his pipe in a fat armchair. Suitably aloof, he was nevertheless well disposed to his children's friends, and when giving out pocket money might include them in his largesse.

Hannah is remembered as petite, attractive and well groomed, more temperamental than her husband, and more approachable. Kate's friends would confide troubles to her over cups of tea in her large and well ordered kitchen.

Otherwise, left alone, Kate and friends would "cook a meat curry or chow mein or something and have a bottle of Pomagne or cider. . . It's repulsive when I think back, we used to put curry and crispy noodles together, and then we used to slice a banana and put it on top, and then put segments of orange on top of that. . ." And if the coast was clear they might also "pinch sherry out of her dad's bottles". And "at weekends we used to sort of grab snacks and that, or do ourselves some soup, and take it up to the den."

"[Kate's] den was like a secret room. You opened what looked like a cupboard door in the upstairs corridor and saw another door across a narrow passage."

"It really was a heap. And we loved it. There was a big open fireplace and we used to have a fire burning and we tried to toast marshmallows but they always used to burn – foul smell! The window was right over the kitchen, and when we were feeling a little bit naughty we used to open it and scream out our favourite songs."

Adults entered the den by invitation only. For this was Kate's place, where she dreamed at leisure, wrote her own poetry and painted butterflies on the walls, and read Tolkien and John Wyndham, and digested brother Paddy's extensive record collection.

She would also take her friends to the family seaside home in Birchington: a pretty, detached house in a road giving onto the sea. An uncommercialised resort (a kind of suburbia-on-sea) with a peaceful bay and chalk cliffs topped with grass walks from which to watch the exquisite sunsets.

A well-to-do family. But it's not the amount of money or property which strikes me about her upbringing. Rather the quality of the relationships this affluence was used to create. Not her considerable spending and pocket money, but the attitude to money in her house.

"[Kate] just asked for money and she got it: whenever she wanted, any money. And her father used to leave his change on the bedside table or downstairs, he used to leave it in various places, and she just used to take it, you know, it was for her to take."

And the licence given her to explore herself:

"She had a lot of freedom in her own way, you know she never had to worry about asking permission really."

You might also easily misjudge her disquieting way of looking at you. Depersonalised. It seems to say: I'm not here. And might imply a kind of violent corollary: neither are you. A way of encountering people without locking into them – which seems almost to deny their existence. What one exasperated writer called her "huge, defensive smile". Unlike Hannah Bush who acknowledges, confronts and engages you eye to eye, psyche to psyche, Kate's gaze is soft (almost un-) focused. She takes you all in while extinguishing the random sparks or cues which might let *you* in. Murderously passive?

I can understand the suspicion and resentment she aroused at school. A reaction this unusually generous schoolgirl, who loved to organise presentations and give presents, couldn't fathom.*

"She was so nice it was ridiculous. So nice. She was really, really nice. I've never met anyone like her." (Schoolfriend)

Sometimes I sort of physically went to push her away. She was, she used to, I used to get frustrated quite a lot you know, she was so inoffensive and so frail and small, you just want to get them out of your sight, you know, and you think, oh. get out of the way." (Schoolfriend)

She was like a sparrow, a tiny delicate little thing with a sweet little face. Not beautiful, but there was something about her. Her sweet voice – people would go, 'Oh God!', 'Yuk!'" (Schoolfriend)

"I was very bombastic. Now I think back at it I was really horrible to her sometimes, you know. I used to get terribly miserable, moody, and sometimes

*Among many stories of her generosity is this from Diane Carman: "I was in hospital, but it wasn't so much the illness as afterwards, I was very weak. I was in a wheelchair for a long time. I couldn't eat anything for weeks. I was so ill I used to have a collar on. I was like a zombie. I couldn't focus my eyes on anything properly. My mum would say, 'It's Catherine Bush,' and I would say, 'Oh hello.' She would come round and shove an LP in my hand with a card that everybody had signed. She sort of organised it all. She used to come in and sit with me and that."

I would pick at her for nothing. She would never, you know, sort of call me names or anything like that. And in the evenings, we used to go round and get this dog, used to take him out for a walk over Fanny on the Hill. And, you know, she was just content to take this dog for a walk all night long. I used to get so frustrated, I used to think, I want to do something else, I have been doing this every single night. But she was quite happy doing that." (Schoolfriend)

"I was jealous of her. So petite and so pretty. A perfect little goody-goody." (Schoolfriend)

"I felt so wicked, I used to be embarrassed to talk to her because I treated her so rotten sometimes. I think I always had the feeling that she'd explode in my face. She never did but I always thought one of these days you're going to say something, go up, really scream and rant and rave . . ." (Schoolfriend)

And Kate:

"[School] was a very cruel environment and I was a loner. But I learnt to get hurt and I learnt to cope with it. My friends used to play this game whereby they'd send you to Coventry. My friends sometimes used to ignore me completely and that would really upset me badly. I felt weak a lot of the time, but I think I was much stronger than I realised."

Her "passivity" and "niceness" have also aroused much hostility from the press. Unfairly. And dishonestly. Because I think these journalists, like her schoolfriends, are actually frustrated and angered (threatened?) by their own aggression, turbulence and insecurity – by their own motives and desires which they read in her attentive eyes and project onto her quiescence. They also construe her disposition through their own psychology, mistaking the absence of their own tensions for her lack of substance.

And miss the interesting fact that her psychology is markedly and qualitatively different from many people's. That many psychological formations, strategies and devices of ambivalence, aggressivity and ego survival are simply not in her. I'm in no position to psychoanalyse her (and in any case I'm confining these remarks to what is pertinent to her work) but let's say that as a child she was *traumatised by affection*. Bonded and formed by profound and pleasurable intimacies, by the undisguised and *unconditional* warmth and trust of her family circle.

Which leaves her, as she's often remarked, extremely vulnerable. For I've also seen her on "home ground" with an unguarded look and was surprised (actually quite shocked) by her rawness of expression – and by the hurt it contained. I understood then the desperation of her need to fence her privacy around. "No strangers feet/will enter me," she entreats in "Get Out

[79]

of My House". And none of her several (and conflicting) explanations of that song account for its *fury*. Which is also a measure of her exceptional courage. And loneliness. Which also goes back a long way.

> *"A word could not harm me*
> *A stone could not bruise me.*
> *A gun could not shoot me*
> *For I am not here."*
> *(Catherine Bush, Form II, school magazine)*

> *"I have noticed him seven times or more*
> *But he has not seen me .*
> *He may have seen a girl called by*
> *My name –*
> *But neither he, nor anyone else will*
> *Ever really see ME."*
> *(Catherine Bush, Form II, school magazine)*

She withdrew into an intense and painful shyness. And ultimately into her work. This direction, thanks mainly to her father, who played jazz piano and showed her middle C – when she's recalled the piano suddenly became alive, an arena for her loneliness. Her father nurtured her talent and listened helpfully to her early compositions. This cohesive family also held musical soirées – both brothers were adept at folk guitar and performed in local folk clubs, and Kate's mother, as a girl, had been a semi-professional Irish folk dancer.

Kate Bush:

"I wasn't an easy, happy go lucky girl because I used to think about everything so much and I think I probably still do. I was writing songs from the age of ten – and I was never really into going to discos and dances and stuff. Obviously I used to like to go and meet boys, but I mainly just liked playing the piano. I never told anyone at school that I did that because I feared it would alienate me even more."

There is one anecdote she often tells about her childhood:

"My father has told me I used to dance to the music on the telly. I remember it vaguely. It was completely unselfconscious and I wasn't aware of people looking at me. One day some people came into the room, saw me and laughed and from that moment I stopped doing it. I think maybe I've been trying to get back there ever since."

Such incidents occur in many biographies of performers as key moments or painful memories which crystallise the childhood choice of a self. For I guess that when around 15 years ago little Cathy Bush froze in her living room in the laughter of outsiders, it dawned on her for the first time that her apparently boundless and formless spontaneity, her unencumbered flux of self-expression, her freedom, could be *seen*, witnessed and judged, bounded and formed by others – that she existed as the object of others' attention. She lost herself. And wanted herself back. With an intensity few realised. And underneath the agonisingly blushing, retiring, and "pigeon-toed" schoolgirl her friends recall she had already formulated her adult self. Orientated the career of her personality towards subtly and magically controlling the object she appeared as in other people's eyes. But meanwhile she lacked a technique and career appropriate to this project.

"She was very, very shy. I remember she had a crush on this boy, first boy she ever had a crush on, she used to call him Gilmour. We used to see him over Fanny on the Hill when we were walking the dog, you know, and we used to walk for hours and hours hoping to catch a glimpse in the freezing cold just in case he was walking across there. I think she only spoke to him once and that was about it. Kate, she was so shy she would go terribly red, really red." (Diane Carman)

"She had a way of speaking when there was a lot of people. In the common room she would look down a lot when she was talking, as if to say, don't look at me . . . She used to smile and keep her teeth closed and her shoulders used to go – it was more of a giggle than an outright laugh. And then, if she really thought something was funny, she'd open her mouth wide and roll her head back. It was still a sort of giggle. And all her arms and legs would go like this – she used to screw them up, bring her knees right up. It was really infectious once she started off." (Schoolfriend)

And a friend of her adolescence recalls that rather than meet her boyfriend Al Buckle in the local pub and "face everybody", she would sometimes leave a flower on his motorbike "to show him she'd been around". And when she played Al her first demo tape she left the room.

These friends were later astonished by the furious discipline with which she mastered her body and expression through dance, mime and vocal training. A discipline to anticipate, contain and finally to control others. Hence her penetrating and manipulative ambivalence about seeing and being seen, a panic between public and private selves characteristic of strongly motivated performers. She will either neutralise you by dissolving her presence in a polite fog, or *drown* you from the stage in the drama, force and integrity of her appearance. "When I perform," she says, "I'm definitely someone else. She's a lot stronger and I wouldn't be as daring as her." Kate Bush is Cathy Bush's revenge.

Kate in front of East Wickham Farm.

And here too is the secret of her formidable and deeply rooted wilfulness – which often astonishes those lulled by her tractable manner.

"I found it very frustrating being treated like a child when I wasn't thinking like a child. I felt I was being patronised, right through until I was 18 or 19. From the age of 10 I felt old." (Kate Bush)

"She really can't conceive of being crossed – only opposed. Which opposition will always give in to her reasonable demands." (EMI executive)

"[Her hair has] got a lot of bounce in it, a lot of body and it's strong hair, wilful hair. It's got a mind of its own her hair. I doubt if she could do much with it if she wanted to. It's unruly." (Kirsty Climo, make-up artist)

So we can now understand the only impluse in her which can overwhelm her generosity. Which leads her to remark that strangers writing about her is "a great intrusion, a kind of violation". And allows her to impose conditions on other professionals in her business which she herself would find impertinent, if not outrageous. Her ructions with photographers especially (and significantly) are legion. And she's taken the drastic (and I think ethically dubious) step of asking them to sign contracts which makes any use of their pictures conditional on *her* approval. It may be her face but it's *their* work. And while many photographers despise and refuse such contracts, the less well known or weaker can lose considerable income – not to mention integrity.*

Kate (far left) with Al Buckle (second from left) throws confetti at a friend's wedding in 1975. Al was Kate's first serious boyfriend. They met at a local youth club and went steady for a year before Kate's strong sense of vocation separated them. "In the past," recalls Kate, "I've had several boyfriends who found it hard to accept that I'm a very creative person. They thought I was a threat to their masculinity."

*Such abuse of power is not unusual in pop where petty bourgeois attitudes make for social naivety about the apparatus which sustains the pop star's talent. And where any "outside" contribution or interpretation is condemned as "exploitation". And pop stars and their managements often walk a fine line between petulance and censorship with blithe talk about what is, or is not, "official" information.

Peaceable and rigorously self-disciplined, burningly shy and with an oddly contrasting pliancy of approach and rigid purpose – this is the fertile psychological ground her art grew from.

Now add her taste for mystery, the thrill of "strange phenomena" – imbibed from her Roman Catholic mother, and the atmosphere of her convent school.

"When I was little my mother fainted for no apparent reason. My father was there and put her on the bed, but he couldn't feel any pulse so he started doing artificial respiration and so on to try to revive her. Meanwhile, according to my mum, she'd taken off like a balloon and hit the ceiling. She was looking down from there at my father pushing her body about and she was calling out 'Leave me alone, I'm all right!'

"Then I walked in asking 'Where's my mum?' and when she saw me she dropped back down into her body, she says, anyway she did come back to life."

". . . school was obviously quite religious in nature being a convent school. I started getting concepts of God very early on. I remember saying to my father that maybe God was a circle because I'd been told that He never began and He never finished. To me that was a circle. A lot of Catholicism is still in me, deeper than I can see."*

"[Kate's school had] old wooden floors and that. And there was a really funny smell, every time we used to go into the old building. It was really strange, especially down by the library. It was very dark. . . I suppose it was the wood, the polish. It always sounded hollow, you know, very strange. And however much you tried to tiptoe along there you still made clanking noises." (Schoolfriend)

"We had to clear out this old room for her den. And we found a big glass bottle with a stopper. Kate stopped me opening it. She thought evil spirits would come out." (Old friend)

"We used to have parties in the den. We used to invite six or seven people, four or five of them would stay the night . . . We used to light candles up there. Frankincense. Get them burning a bit. We used to sit there with some spooky music and read ghost stories." (Diane Carman)

"I often find myself inspired by unusual, distorted and weird subjects, as opposed to things that are straightforward. It's a reflection of me, my liking for weirdness." (Kate Bush)

Hence her feeling for eccentric tangents and vague discordances of mood

---

*I've discussed Kate's Catholicism in some detail with reference to Johnny Rotten's but only by way of contrasting the images (not the personalities) of these two, see "When Malcolm Laughs" in Fred and Judy Vermorel, *Sex Pistols,* revised edition, 1981. I think their Catholicism gave both these very different artists an extremism and expressive edge over their contemporaries. And considered together Kate and John give an insight into the tensions bubbling underneath late '70s Britain, which later exploded out of art into such events as the 1980-81 youth riots.

Kate (bottom row, second left) in her first year at St Joseph's Convent Grammar School.

and effect. Which can work admirably in music and dance. But less so when it surfaces in literary flirtations with the occult or such low grade philosophers as Gurdjieff. A naivety which does however testify to her intact "sense of wonder" – without which, said Heidegger, no genuine philosopy or poetry is possible.*

So by the time she was 16 her isolation, father's encouragement and catalyst of her brothers' interest in folk, rock and poetry – Jay (John Carder Bush) is a practising and published poet – had considerably matured her talent. At this stage Dave Gilmour of Pink Floyd was persuaded to listen to her earliest demos and was impressed enough to pay for three professional demos produced by Andrew Powell at Air Studio. These were heard by Bob Mercer of EMI. Then by Terry Slater, a wily, gum-chewing old rocker (who also first signed the Sex Pistols) and one of EMI's brighter executives.

"I was just passing by Bob Mercer's office one day and I heard a demo tape of

*She espouses a vague mixture of humanitarian creeds and motives and is also a vegetarian – out of respect for animals and life. Her dancing as well shows affinity with animals, in the sense of Curt Sachs: "Only in the dance is the mystic bond between animals and man consummated." *(World History of the Dance)*

'Man with the child in his eyes'. I said to Bob, 'Who's that chick?' I literally opened the door to the office and said that to Bob. He said, 'It's a girl called Kate Bush'. I took it from there. I said, 'That's *really* good: how do I get in touch with her?' and I got a number and I called her. She came by the next day: sat right there where you are. She was overwhelmed that somebody would be interested in what she was doing. I asked her about her interests, her ideas and realized she was somebody special, really intriguing. She told me about her dance school. A really dedicated, hard-working, extra special person. She stood out a mile. I had to get involved with her.''

Kate signed recording and publishing contracts with EMI for a modest £3,500 advance and left school in the lower sixth in a flurry of rumour – and with some parental misgivings.

EMI too was nervous and insisted she wait before being launched. Bob Mercer: "On meeting her I realised how young she was mentally. We gave her some money to grow up with." "EMI was like another family for her... [she was] the company's daughter for a few years." A trying and depressing period for Kate, although under Bob Mercer's guidance she did polish her composition and singing. She also gigged in South London pubs with her three piece KT Bush band. And took dance and mime classes – notably under Lindsey Kemp. Which experience gave a decisive focus to her vision of fusing music and movement.

And then her fabled instantaneous success with her first single "Wuthering Heights" in early '78 . . . and the ensuing tale of statistics and superlatives I leave to someone else.

"While we're all aware of looking after each other, we're all very much individuals. We can work as a unit – a very strong unit – but I don't find it inhibiting or over-protective." (Kate Bush)

"They were a shock. I always expect a doctor's family to be run of the mill . . . There was a hothouse atmosphere in there.

"I think of photos of them – standing there looking Pre-Raphaelite and serious. They all seemed to have a kind of separateness about them." (Teresa Fox, Paddy Bush's ex-girlfriend)*

*An oddly "Victorian" family in its mixture of precociousness and innocence, amateurism and determination. The first demo tape sent round by Kate and brothers contained over 50! of Kate's compositions. Not surprisingly it was rejected by every record company. And, despite Kate's shrewd (ex-EMI) personal assistant, Hilary Walker, "Kate Bush" remains an essentially family business.

Still, in her mid-twenties, deeply embroiled in her family plot, living with her brothers and returning and returning to her parents' home where she loves quite simply to spend time in their company. A depth of emotion we don't need her frequent avowals to know about. Just feel the passion of that lovely song: "Warm and Soothing". "I'm afraid by how we grow old."

Suburbia, of course, is founded on family life. Which is another aspect of

Left to right: Hannah Bush, Paddy, Kate and Jay.

its (and her) modernity. For families in general have never been so bonded or enduring as today, and are becoming more so. As every serious study shows – discount journalistic and Vatican folklore! And one of the results of this trend is that children are leaving home physically *and* emotionally later and later. I doubt Kate will ever properly leave home. Why should she? It's her inspiration.

Which also limits her. For I think she's rejected that adaptation to experience and routines outside home, the "secondary socialisation" beyond childhood. Rejected, for example, learning and resists intellectual-isation with slippery panic. Relishing Beefheart's witticism, "he's had too much to think", she seems to feel coherent ideas or thinking might challenge her, cramp her lightness of touch, dull her brightness. Rooted in the dream of a childhood self unencumbered by disputes, factions or decisions. An untainted "core" of feeling, instinct and harmony. A myth.

The myth is her business. But her insularity – her lack of research and disdain of method – does have the effect of letting her skimp ideas which sometimes deserve more attention than she gives them. There are enough ideas on *Never for Ever,* for instance, for three LP's. And enough on *The Dreaming* for five or six. And they're all such good ideas. It would be nice to hear them more extended and sustained. Which might also incline her less towards "originality" which, as an end in itself, is uninteresting.

Kate Bush:

". . . as soon as you get your hands on the production, it becomes your baby. That's really exciting for me, because you do everything for your own child."

"The freedom you feel when you're actually in control of your own music is fantastic."

But *The Dreaming* completely vindicated her insistence on producing herself – which, along with others, I first doubted the wisdom of. And it is this self-production which has changed her from being merely a brilliant songwriter into a major artist.*

For she's taken production beyond the conventional icing on the cake, the gloss to make a pop song "cut". Gone beyond "production values" to make her production as integral to the mood and idea of a piece as its arrangement or lyric. She now elaborately and carefully *composes* production. And with a sensitivity and fluency which puts her in front of everyone. More original than Bowie, more daring than Ferry, more musically competent (as John Taverner also thought) than Pink Floyd, and as sophisticated (and less dry)

---

*Pop lacks an aesthetic. Which limits its development – especially in the innovative area Kate Bush is moving into. The "quality" rock critics borrow an irrelevant vocabulary from classical musicology, a vocabulary perfected before the phonogram and photography were even invented, and which is fatally hooked on quasi-moralistic (good/bad) judgements and schoolmasterly axioms (well done/try harder). Philosophically innocent. The pop papers lack vision and funds to attract much imagination and often depend on virtual groupies paid pocket money to bask in current attractions – whose only "method" is to kick arse or lick arse, whichever yields more (or sassier) copy. The disparity of effort, imagination and intelligence between *The Dreaming* and its reviews was routinely appalling. We were given opinions – these people wouldn't know you can have anything else, all very smart and brisk and, if at all possible, wounding. It was frequently said that *The Dreaming* was "over produced" – this from people who wouldn't know EQ from a bicycle clip. The notable exception was Chris Thomas in *Practical HiFi*, November '82 – but then he's a producer not a journalist. A poverty of debate which also surrounded Peter Gabriel's simultaneously released *Peter Gabriel 4*. Now it's well established from other arts that artists are not always the best people to discuss their work. Frequently it's their very inarticulacy and closed vision which drives them. So they sometimes need overviews and alternative insights. Just as audiences sometimes need helping over the gap between what they expect and what is offered. What a pity the rock press didn't rise to the occasion. What else is it for?

than Gabriel.

Now self-production is a schizophrenic trick. For the calculation, distance and focus a producer needs clash with the urgency, closeness and rawness a performer needs to keep boiling in front of a mike. And there's a danger the artist/producer will slow and stale the artist/performer or the performer over-excite the producer. While Kate listens for the "vibes" (as she puts it) in Abbey Road's Studio Two, she necessarily neglects other vibes which only show on dials. So how does she manage?

Let's take "The Dreaming", her most complex production so far, and a masterpiece of mood: a Kubrick movie in sound with not a note, word or whisper out of place, and mixed with transitions folding in and out as smoothly as flesh. It's also simple: direct and immediately felt, and seems to happen all at once – as only the best work does.*

It was the least pre-planned track on the album, starting without lyrics as "the Abo track" – an idea to do something aboriginal. Kate put down a percussion pattern inspired by aboriginal sounds in her small home studio with a Linn drum machine. She then brought the demo into the Townhouse Studio, re-recorded the Linn on to 24 track, played in piano and laid down three tracks of guide vocal to establish the structure. The piano was then sent through a harmoniser one octave up, and again (for stereo effect) almost an octave up, and then sent to a harmonised echo plate which fed back on and on itself to give its haunted quality. Two drummers elaborated Kate's Linn pattern with a big bass drum and variety of other drums, especially toms. African drums were tried but found disappointing until miked inside as well as out (and put slightly out of phase) and satisfactorily EQed. Delay effects were also used to enhance the impact of the main drum accent. Other drums, suitably dulled, and snare drums without snares filled the percussion out, which was tracked and tracked and bounced down and tracked again, etc, to achieve that impressively solid and strangely elastic boom. The sharp percussive sound was made by rhythmically smashing two pieces of marble in the Townhouse's "live" stone room. These gradually splintered adding extraneous sounds which were gated out. Other percussion effects were also explored, bemusing the canteen staff who wondered why Kate Bush wanted their pots and pans, and also the navvies whose nearby building site was looted for odd pieces of timber. Finally, a stage was reached where the Linn could be dispensed with but as the sound was just better with it in, it stayed –

*I also like "The Dreaming" for avoiding the pomposity of a white girl's burden or the looting of so-called "primitive" cultures fashionable in some rock circles. Her respect for her sources is easy to hear and feel. "The Dreaming" is the dream of an entire continent, mined by violence, but still swarming with magic. A beautiful work.

just.

This painstaking, step-by-step and meticulous experimentation is typical of how she works. Beginning with a conventional (and usually fairly complete) home-produced demo, she follows every possibility and suggestion to its limit, often abandoning effects as "not working" after hours or days of work. She's wary of "self-indulgence" and in the end the criterion is whether something "communicates". She also works in close rapport with her engineers, and has been lucky enough to find several very talented ones. Interestingly, while discussing the work she often uses visual rather than musical terms, suggesting, for example, a sound become "darker", "rounder", "redder" or "bigger".

She has greatly matured and extended her vocal style, burying the shrill little girl and refining her technique into an emotional spectrum as discriminated as Schoenberg's *Stimmung*. She uses her voice primarily as an instrument for emotion (hence the often heard complaint "I can't hear the words"), imagining and living out a role, and what comes most directly from her performance stays on tape.

And she's strangled the sweet darling of former lyrics. Learnt to re-write: re-search, re-think and re-cast her words. Not merely as style or reach-me-down intonation, but through an impressive grasp of the modern writer's problem now that electronic media have usurped naturalistic dialogue, narration and rhetoric. When "spontaneity" is the biggest bluff of all. And without being laboured or recherché her lyrics can achieve a lovingly sculpted presence as sensuously disciplined as D H Lawrence's poetry and as chidingly ironic as Jacques Prévert, but with a reflexive tension both these writers lack.

She's also been able to develop her subtle sound symbolism –previously most striking in the uncanny drawing back of the rifle bolt in "Army Dreamers" – by using a Fairlight, the remarkable computer synthesizer which can turn any sound, from a whisper to the smash of glass, into a complete harmonic scale which can then be played on keyboard. The orchestral chord which punctuates "The Dreaming" was found already in the Fairlight's "memory". And the unusual snare sound on "Get Out of My House" was elaborately made from the sound of violently slamming doors.

She's also absorbed Peter Gabriel's percussive experiments and turned them into her own percussive *desperation*. No longer the *enfant gâté* of "Wuthering Heights" but a woman who has lived and suffered. So her rhythms explode, let you drop – and catch you on the up beat – a curious mix of vulnerability and force which can transport you with the eerie, disarming and impossible momentum of "Suspended in Gaffa", or lose you in an intricate cannonade and percussive veil: emotionally very fraught and technically very innovative. Which with her uniquely intimate fusion of performance and production makes it seem as if her whole body and soul is gargling, spitting, crackling, screaming and spilling out inside you.

"Get Out of My House" and "Leave it Open" also have a histrionic demonism reminiscent of that rather neglected composer, Bernard Herrmann, who wrote several Hitchcock movie scores, including the hair-raising score for *Marnie*.

She's at her best when unconstrained by narrative or conventional song forms. For she's an instinctive surrealist, a conjurer who can snatch moods out of thin air and make instant theatre in the listener's head.

Eyes pop and you're in a knot. Her dancing looks artless, almost clumsy, arch *and* gauche. But it's as telling as a Balinese temple girl's. Only Kate's wrists and elbows flick with a language of childhood: where discomfit and embarrassment melt, lope, canter, fly in the panto flash and thunder of dishevelled sentimentality: legs bow, hips locomote and Kate on a hot tin roof vanishes in her smoke of arms. Also a garish come-on which reminds me of the private and twisted body symbolism of what used to be called "hysterical" patients you see illustrated in old psychology text books. And a stagey freedom of crotch you may find vulgar, which it is, but so was Diaghilev.

Terry Slater, EMI:
"Kate is a real English girl, she's from the roots of Great Britain. It's not a gimmick or produced. She's the first really *English* girl singer for a long time."
Kate Bush:
"'Everything I do is very English and I think that's one reason I've broken through to a lot of countries. The English vibe is very appealing."

[92]

"This house is full of m-m-madness."
(Kate Bush, "Get Out of My House")

A very English madness. As English as Delius – as sweet and erotic (and her "Delius" is almost aphrodisiac). As Vaughan Williams' fulsomely mellow pastorales. Because she's partly rooted like them in the nostalgic gentlemanly vision of English folk defined by Victorian collectors and interpreted from Percy Grainger to Ewan MacColl. A slightly preachy, frail and cosy tradition.

As English as her father's status: a suburban doctor. The inheritor of his social neutrality, professional assuredness and proprietary good sense. She wears her culture like her clothes: loose and comfortable. She fits.

But not exactly. For she's also an Irish rose. Which gives her distance and keenness to cut through British complacency and go beyond her culture. Into madness. To reach genius: "Oh England My Lionheart", what a pure and insane madrigal.

Even so, I do feel her Irish moods are an *intellectual* reference, more calculated than her impulsive, resurgent lyricism. Nor are her songs cyclical or ornamental. And she lacks that crystalline pathos Irish performers find so easily. An Irish head, maybe, but an English soul. Hannah the law-giver, but Dr Bush is this Leo's lionheart.

But what's nice is that she's English without that supercilious greyness of so many English artists. And no snob.

Kate Bush:
"I think everyone is emotional and I think a lot of people are afraid of being so. They feel that it's vulnerable. Myself I feel it's the key to everything and that the more you can find out about your emotions the better."

Unusually sensuous, unusually generous. She wants to make us happy. Give us everything she has all at once. Superbly courageous, on a high wire over ridicule, disdainful of her own safety, always ready to risk her talent and herself. She opens her heart with her mouth and throws herself at us with frightened urgency and that half anxious curl of her upper lip – as if fearful of finding nothing on our side. And we would be most ungracious if she didn't. If we didn't respond to her warmth and vulnerability with some vulnerability ourselves.

Kate Bush is a profoundly *subversive* artist.

DISCOGRAPHY

ALBUMS		
EMC 3223	THE KICK INSIDE	February 1978
EMA 787	LIONHEART	December 1978
EMA 794	NEVER FOR EVER	September 1980
EMC 3419	THE DREAMING	September 1982
SINGLES		
EMI 2719	WUTHERING HEIGHTS/Kite	January 1978
EMI 2806	THE MAN WITH THE CHILD IN HIS EYES/Moving	May 1978
EMI 2887	HAMMER HORROR/Coffee Homeground	November 1978
EMI 2911	WOW/Full House	March 1979
MIEP 2991	KATE BUSH ON STAGE (LIVE EP) THEM HEAVY PEOPLE/DON'T PUSH YOUR FOOT ON THE HEARTBREAK/JAMES AND THE COLD GUN/L'AMOUR LOOKS SOMETHING LIKE YOU	September 1979
EMI 5058	BREATHING/The Empty Bullring	April 1980
EMI 5085	BABOOSHKA/Ran Tan Waltz	June 1980
EMI 5106	ARMY DREAMERS/Delius/Passing Through The Air	September 1980
EMI 5121	DECEMBER WILL BE MAGIC AGAIN/ Warm and Soothing	November 1980
EMI 5201	SAT IN YOUR LAP/Lord of The Reedy River	June 1981
EMI 5296	THE DREAMING/Dreamtime (Instrumental Version)	July 1982

VIDEO

TVD 90 0503 2	KATE BUSH LIVE	Hammersmith Odeon Concert, May 13 1979

Acknowledgements

Thanks first of all to Judy Vermorel who did the interviews and additional research, and thought it all through with me; then Nick Launay; Liz Bull; the staffs of: the Essex Records Office (superbly efficient matriarchy!), Friends House Library, Colchester Local History Library, Halstead Local History Society, Public Record Office, St Catherine's House, Somerset House, the Society of Genealogists, the London Library, British Museum Library, Colindale Newspaper Library, and Westminster Central Reference Library; for Pebmarsh: Norman Brown, Jack Cook, George Courtauld, Eileen and Pete Daws of the Kings Head, Mr and Mrs Frank, Mrs Holmes, the Rev. S Hough, Bertie Hunt, Beatrice Page, Betty Pearson, the Potter family and George Trendell; for South Ockenden: Mrs Bailey, Milly Boreham, Violet Blows, Mr and Mrs Cook, the Rev. Stanley Davis, Mr and Mrs Faraway, Mrs Morris, Mr and Mrs Page, the Philips family, Queenie Rainbird, Mrs Smith and Pastor A J Smithers; for specialist advice: Jack Baxter of the Essex Marriage Index, Brian Benson, Judy Louwns and Myrtle Solomon, the Royal Geographical Society and Hertfordshire College of Agriculture and Horticulture; also the incumbents of the parishes of Great and Little Maplestead, Finchingfield and Castle Hedingham, and the charming couple who run the Halstead Wimpy bar for many restorative cups of tea; for Welling: Adele Beckley, Francis Byrne, Diane Carman, Sarah Craddy, Teresa Fox, Fiona Gent, Catherine Hellier, John Hooper, Eleanor Lapore, Sheila Mubi, Anne Paice and Jane Robbins; for EMI: Bob Mercer and Terry Slater; and also Kirsty Climo; and for lending me their musical ears: John Taverner and Tim McDonald.

Additional picture credits

Front cover Clive Arrowsmith, *back cover* Pebmarsh churchyard, Fred Vermorel, *Pages 2-3* London Features International Ltd, *6-7* Pebmarsh tree, Fred Vermorel, *8* BBC, *10 & 11* London Features International Ltd, *14-15* Fred Vermorel, *20 top* London Express Newspapers, *30-31* courtesy of Tyne Tees Television, *32* London Features International, *41* Pete Still, *53* BBC, *54* BBC, *59 bottom right* Pete Still, *65* S Skelly/Daily Telegraph, *68* S Skelly/Daily Telegraph, *69* BBC, *72* Pete Still, *74 left* London Express, *75* BBC Hulton Picture Library, *76 & 77* S Skelly/Daily Telegraph, *80* S Skelly/Daily Telegraph, *83* BBC Hulton Picture Library, *88* BBC Hulton Picture Library, *95* Pete Still.